I0024329

James H. Keeling

Quæro

some questions in matter, energy, intelligence, and evolution.

James H. Keeling

Quæro
some questions in matter, energy, intelligence, and evolution.

ISBN/EAN: 9783337367510

Printed in Europe, USA, Canada, Australia, Japan

Cover: Foto ©Andreas Hilbeck / pixelio.de

More available books at **www.hansebooks.com**

QUÆRO

[SOME QUESTIONS IN MATTER, ENERGY, INTELLIGENCE, AND EVOLUTION.]

BY

JAMES H. KEELING, M.D.

("BACILLUS")

AUTHOR OF "SONG OF A SQUIRT," ETC.,

LATE LECTURER ON GYNÆCOLOGY IN THE
UNIVERSITY COLLEGE OF SHEFFIELD.

With Diagrams.

"HOMINIS EST PROPRIA VERI INQUISITIO."

FOR PRIVATE CIRCULATION.

LONDON:
PRINTED BY TAYLOR AND FRANCIS, RED LION COURT, FLEET STREET.
1898.

ALERE FLAMMAM.

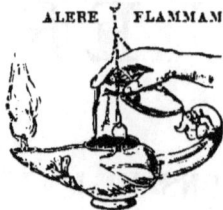

PRINTED BY TAYLOR AND FRANCIS,
RED LION COURT, FLEET STREET.

With the
        Author's Compliments.

PREFACE.

THE following pages are taken from an un-
published essay. Separated from their context
they are somewhat fragmentary, but this is of
no moment if they remain readable. The first
two chapters were contributed to a Volume
issued last year, by professors and teachers in
the University College of Sheffield, in com-
memoration of the recent incorporation of that
Institution. The third and fourth chapters
have not appeared before.

In his admirable " Foundations of Belief,"
Mr. Balfour includes, under the term
" Naturalism," all those forms of thought,
philosophic or scientific, which are usually
held to be antagonistic to religion. Of these,

Materialism is perhaps the oldest. Its significance has varied, in different ages, with the varying conceptions of Nature ; but it has proved very tenacious of life and, in a modern form, is still widely extant.

Owing to intrinsic excellence, and as the work of an eminent and busy statesman, Mr. Balfour's book at once arrested attention, and drew forth much laudatory comment. Here and there, however, a hostile voice was raised ; amongst the rest that of Professor Huxley, whose criticism was commenced in the "Nineteenth Century" for March, 1895. It was never finished. Before its completion, death had robbed us of one of our most gifted and vigorous scientists.

He would be a bold man who should undertake to wield the club which dropped from Huxley's grasp. Indeed there are some who think the Professor himself had become less belligerent, and that, had he lived a few years longer, he would ultimately have found, like Spencer and Romanes, a peaceful meeting-ground for science and religion. But of such a tryst, combative materialism will at present hear nothing. It asserts there is less prospect of peace than ever, in view of the support gained (as is thought) from the later advances of physical and biologic science ; especially from that luminous view of Evolution which we owe to the genius of Darwin. In what follows, an attempt is made to ascertain whether this opinion is well-founded, or not.

With respect to the physiological data in the third chapter, the writer has to express his thanks for the kind supervision of Dr. A. Hall, Professor of Physiology in the University College.

267 Glossop Road, Sheffield,
      May, 1898.

CONTENTS.

CHAPTER I.

IS EVOLUTION AUTOMATIC?

"Felix, qui potuit rerum cognoscere causas."

(Part of a conversation overheard in Sheffield.)

E. (Enquirer). So you turn our old friend, Nature, into an Automaton—limitless, self-maintaining, ruled by innate forces, its material basis engaged by these forces in endless alternating evolution and devolution, and having an existence to which no term can be assigned either in the past or future—a grand automaton no doubt, but nothing more.

M. (Materialist). My view, I believe, is endorsed by science. Matter can neither be destroyed nor originated by any known force. Forever changing in form, it never varies in sum, and never ceases to exist. In like

B

manner, the energy associated with matter, though subject to constant transformation, is neither lost nor diminished.

E. What do we really know about matter? Of its varieties and properties, much; of its structure, something; of its essential nature, of its origin and destiny, absolutely nothing. On these points you have had undeniable authority, and I will merely remind you of what Professor Tait said—"we do not know, and are probably incapable of discovering, what matter *is*"; and again, "We advisedly use the word *structure* instead of *nature*, for it must be repeated, till it is fully accepted, that the discovery of the ultimate nature of matter is probably beyond the range of human intelligence." (The italics are his. See "Properties of Matter," 3rd edition, 1894, pp. 16–17.) Then as to duration. You are entitled to say matter is imperishable under *existing* conditions, not under *any* conditions. Our knowledge of past and future conditions is far too limited to permit of our assuming the everlasting duration of matter. As we have seen, scientific opinion differs on the point: some think it certain, others only probable; some regard it as improbable, many as incapable of either proof or disproof; another view is that what is now known as matter will ultimately be looked on as merely a mode of energy.

M. Matter must be taken as we find it. As to its indestructibility, the testimony of chemistry and physics is conclusive: geology and astronomy are equally positive as to its existence for countless ages. To reason from what is known to what is probable is certainly in accordance with scientific usage.

E. Yes, but not the building up of a pseudo-scientific hypothesis, as I think it, on a foundation of which a notable part is at once so essential and so precarious. But I am not surprised at your pertinacity. For me, the eternity or non-eternity of matter is of no consequence, but for you it is vital. If matter be not eternal, it had a beginning, and you are ruined. For then, since you admit no thing nor power outside of matter, nor antecedent to it, you have to evolve it and

all its belongings from—nothing; an origin
even more hopeless than that 'spontaneous
generation' of living organisms which science
denies, although there is then present at least
something to start from.   As, however, your
postulate does not affect me, it shall be
conceded.   Of course it is not enough : if
matter were eternal and nothing more, it
might have remained for ever in its primal
homogeneity.   How does it emerge from
this ?

M. Obviously by impulse from the energy
which dwells in it.

E. Then you make energy an attribute
of matter.   This is scarcely admitted by
science.   It is usual to speak of matter *and*
energy.   Matter one thing, energy another.
Energy always associated with matter no
doubt ; but not always with the *same* matter :
on the contrary, " continually passing from
one portion of matter to another," and " doing
work " (Clerk Maxwell, " Matter and Motion,"
1891).   In contrast with this, a leading
characteristic of matter, as laid down in the
text-books, is ' inertia.'

M. So long as matter is acknowledged to be the constant partner of energy, I care nothing for its technical inertness. Listen to this passage from your favourite Tait ("Properties of Matter," p. 7)—" There is, however, a most important point to be noticed. Energy is never found except in association with matter. Hence we might define matter as the *Vehicle* or *Receptacle of Energy*; and it is already more than probable that energy will ultimately be found, in all its varied forms, to depend upon *Motion* of matter" (the italics and capitals are his). Mark, energy to depend on motion, not motion on energy. The statement just quoted has, I believe, the full sanction of science, and its significance is great. It enounces, first, a scientific certainty, viz., the invariable association of energy and matter; second, the strong scientific probability that energy in all its forms is dependent on the motion of matter. The view, indeed, is rapidly gaining ground that all forms of energy—heat, light, electricity, chemic action, &c.—are mere modifications of motion.

E. We have been over that ground, and you will remember that science knows as little of the origin and cause of motion as it does of the origin and nature of matter. Even Newton had to take matter as 'a going concern,' without ascertaining the nature and source of the assets. Science tells us *how* matter moves, and has laid down the laws of motion : *why* it moves, why in a particular way, she does not pretend to know. However, I quite recognise the importance of motion and all its modes. How do you apply it?

M. In this way. Whether dated from forever or from a beginning, there is, so far as we know, no such thing as motionless matter, and never has been. When its movement is no longer evident to unaided sense, the chemist is there to demonstrate the unceasing play of the elements ; the physicist, to tell us of the ever-trembling ether, and the probably constant vibration of the molecules of even the hardest solids; and the astronomer, to point out the ceaseless flight of suns and planets. The term 'resting,' as

applied to matter, is technical only. The
'motion' or 'rest' of any given portion of
matter is relative to the position of another
portion, which is itself moving. A stone
'rests' on the ground; they are moving
together, and with extreme velocity. Besides
having axial rotation, our earth is moving
in its orbit at a speed of 18 miles per
second. Our sun, with his planets, is held
to be travelling towards Vega at a rate,
variously estimated, of from 6 to 16 miles
per second, and he is slow compared with
certain other suns. In view of this incessant
atomic, molecular, and translational movement, I claim the right to speak of motion
as an inalienable possession or characteristic
of matter. Add, now, the extreme scientific
probability that this motion of matter is at
the root of all forms of energy, and what you
are pleased to call my Automaton is nearly
equipped. One further touch only is needed.
Let energy be applied to develop as well
as move, and the evolution of the universe is
secured.

E. You are going back to the materialism

of Moleschott and Büchner; this was more
esteemed forty or fifty years ago than it is
now.   Then you have blended your two
factors, matter and energy, in a way which
science does not at present ratify.   So far as
our argument is concerned, this is of no
consequence ; we may say energy *and* matter,
or energy *of* matter, or we may combine the
two, and speak of *energised matter*.[1]   I have
now, however, to remind you that, in con-
structing your automaton, you have entirely
lost sight of a third factor, viz., that consummate intelligence which, unless our reason
perpetually plays us false, is so conspicuous
in the mechanism of the universe.   From the
first we ruled out Chance; order and law are
everywhere, and   chance   does   not   produce

---

[1] According to an important book, by Singer and
Berens, which has appeared lately (1897), it seems
likely that current scientific views about matter and
energy may have to be revised.   See " Some Unrecog-
nized Laws of Nature," pp. 113–123.   The possibility
of impending change may also be gathered from certain
passages in the magnificent monograph on " Electric
Movement in Air and Water " recently published by
Lord Armstrong.   See also his letter to the " Times "
of Aug. 26th, 1897.

these. Nor can we seriously regard them as
the mere products or inventions of human
thought. No doubt this has been suggested.
A ribald wit has even said, 'the heavens
declare the glory of Newton, and the firma-
ment sheweth his handywork.' Had anyone,
in like manner, asserted that the marvels of
biology declare the glory of Darwin, none
would have been more astonished than
Darwin himself. Most people I fancy will
regard the human mind as but a feeble and
belated investigator of the previous arrangements of surpassing intelligence, and our
knowledge of the phenomena and laws
of nature as nothing more than the
" approximately successful outcome of endless
guessing " (Karl Pearson).

M. In place of a prior designing intelligence, I put energy and evolution, and can
thus give a more natural and reasonable
account of the universe, whether in its origin
or history.

E. You are entitled to your opinion:
for many, a controlling intelligence is as
indisputable a factor as is matter or energy.

In the early days of evolution, the popular notion was that some new, subtle, and wide-reaching kind of automatism had been discovered, whereby the universe had produced itself, and could maintain and develop itself, independently of any intelligent control. But the vision was premature—due chiefly to the fact that certain votaries of the new cult were too busy applying their novel instrument, and too dazzled by its excellence, to remember that no automaton has ever been found or invented which will commence and go of itself, or which can dispense with constructive intelligence.   As well imagine that a watch can originate itself, arrange its own works, and go without winding.   The blunder has now been rectified, and we need no stronger illustration of the normal tendency of evolution than is supplied by that prince of evolutionists, Herbert Spencer.   All the wonders which evolution has disclosed, all the phenomena of the universe, are traced back, by his disciplined intellect, to a supreme and eternal energy.

M. Precisely where I trace them to.

Evolution is nothing more than a special application of persistent energy.

E. Wait a moment. As Mephistopheles says—

> " Mit Worten lässt sich trefflich streiten,
>   Mit Worten ein System bereiten,
>   An Worte lässt sich trefflich glauben,"

Huxley compared words to 'counters'; I liken them to coin. You may stamp the same image on good metal and base, but that will not make them equal. The coin you are offering has not the same value as Spencer's. Your conception of supreme energy differs essentially from his. Your energy is purely physical—the motion of matter, or derivatives therefrom. His is psychic, as well as physical : the donor of life, therefore itself living, or inclusive of life ; the source of innumerable manifestations of intelligence, therefore itself intelligent, or including intelligence. 'Nemo dat quod non habet.' Your notion of energy needs expanding, but you will never get anything psychic out of the motion of matter. If you are prepared to admit that supreme energy, besides being all-powerful, is also living and intelligent, I can be content. But in so doing, you have given yourself away. My third factor is accepted, and your Automaton goes to pieces: in its place, we have an universe regulated by intelligence, as well as ruled by power.

M. Before admitting your third factor, let us see what the two we have will do. I can give you instances in which both life and mind spring from their operation. Go into the nearest field. There you will find water, carbonic acid, ammonia, and salts turning into grass, grass into sheep, sheep into mutton, which mutton will presently turn into the thinking grey cortex of your brain and mine, and thus enable us to discern the sufficiency of my factors. Take another illustration, the human ovum. A simple cell, not more than $\frac{1}{120}$ of an inch in diameter, the compeers of which, in untold numbers, are daily passing into oblivion as certainly as do the superfluous eggs in the over-fecund roe of a red herring. Yet, fertilise this cell, feed it, environ it suitably, and in nine months it has developed into a bouncing baby seven pounds in weight ; in forty years, it has become a Socrates or Shakespeare. If the womb of woman and forty years of time can yield this astounding result, what may we not expect from the womb of the world in millions of years.

E. You are incorrigible. Nothing will cure you short of stripping away every rag of the stolen garments in which you have clad your factors. We must examine more closely this alleged faculty of self-development.

Put briefly, its meaning and scope may be thus stated :—

Energised matter, which potentially contains, also determines the universe. At first matter is homogeneous, both physically and chemically, and distributed uniformly through space. By virtue of original endowment, it is in motion ; this motion, at first of atoms, becomes molecular- and, ultimately, mass-motion. Impelled by its innate

faculty of development (may Newton
forgive you), matter becomes aggre-
gated into masses, small and large,
and physical homogeneity disappears.
Accompanying this physical change,
there is a chemical one : matter
passes from chemical unity into
elemental diversity, and at length
takes the form of the various elements
which chemists recognise. Thus physically and chemically changed, matter
engages in endless and advancing
combinations, and at last presents
itself as Nature in its inorganic form.
From inorganic matter, by higher
synthesis but under impulse of the
same force, organic substance is
produced. In matter thus become
organic, organisms spring up, vegetal
and animal, and here occurs the
important moment in which life first
appears. Vegetal life pursues its
course simultaneously with animal
life, largely ministering to the latter,
and steadily growing in complexity
and importance ; but we need not
follow its steps, for it is from animal
life that the grand issue comes. When

animal life is once started, there are presently associated with it certain psychic phenomena—sensation, perception, volition, &c.—and to these phenomena, when sufficiently ad - vanced, the term ' mind ' is given. Animal life, like vegetal, is ever pressing onward and upward, and passes through an infinite series of ascending gradations. From unicellular to many-celled organisms, from cells doing everything to cells strictly specialised and grouped in organs, from the lowest invertebrate to the highest, until at length the dignity of a back-bone is reached : then, through fish, reptile, bird, mammal, until the process, emerging by way of the anthropoid apes, culminates in man : man as a low savage at first, but ever advancing, and, in his best strain, capable of, and at last attaining, the highest civilisation.

Such appears to me a fair account of the passage from chaos to ' kosmos ' according to the Materialist, and ascribed by him to that faculty of self-development, resident in matter, which goes by the name of 'evolution.' But this faculty is surely nothing more than our old acquaintance, energy, under a new name. Why should christening him afresh alter him so advantageously?

M. You are perfectly aware that he was 'altered advantageously' before being re-christened. Darwin took care of that. Evolution, though as I think simply a special form of energy, was practically unknown until Darwin discovered it.

E. Any eulogy of Darwin on my part would be an impertinence, and I have far too deep a respect for his genius to accept that automatic caricature, which is all you will ever get out of the motion of matter, as the equivalent of what he meant by evolution. We discussed this some time ago when considering the advent and early history of the elements, and the first appearance of life and mind in nature. Let me remind you briefly of some of our points.

As to the genesis of the elements, we saw

that no merely physical agent—whether Sir
Wm. Crookes's [1] electric 'pendulum,' or any
other mechanical 'differentiator of atoms '—
would suffice.　Clerk Maxwell's 'sorting
demon' is more promising, but the imp
would need to be bigger.　Whatever the
cause, the result was a precise, orderly, final,
chemic and physical discrimination and stamp-
ing of matter previously homogeneous and
uniform.　In the wide interval which separates
azoic rock from nebula, the unceasing play
of energy and matter led to results which
cannot be credited to chance ; and, if they were
automatic, I must ask you for the author of
the mechanism.　Recall, for a moment, what
is included in the evolution of the elements.
Their curious number ;　their singular and
orderly appearance ;　their wonderful variety in

---

[1] See his Lecture at the Royal Institution on the
"Genesis of the Elements," reported in the "Chemical
News " for 1887 (pp. 83–88 and 95–99).　It is scarcely
necessary to say that this eminent chemist, like
Newton, is enquiring *how*, not *whence* or *why*.　Primal
matter (' protyle '), and energy in the form of electricity,
are taken as present.　A similar remark of course
applies to Clerk Maxwell.

C

amount, weight, and properties; their separate-
ness and independence—inviolable, yet har-
monised with a most intricate relationship;
their innumerable combinations and sepa-
rations, yet always by fixed and definite
measure; their permanence and unchanging
identity throughout the ages; their unique
history; their fitness to form sun, planet, star,
or comet—to become mountain, plain, ocean,
or atmosphere—to be the vehicle of life in
its unending manifestations, and take shape
as plant, animal, even as man himself, until
finally they reach their highest place and office
as the thinking matter (according to you) of
his brain; in a word, to form the entire frame-
work in which all the wonders of the universe
are displayed. This is what the outfitting of
the elements means, and this the task your
energy had to accomplish. Was it then
blind?—Was it merely physical—whether
electric or otherwise? Was there no intelligence, no wisdom, no foresight in this ordering
of the elements, millions of years ago, so that
they should now have worked out such a
stupendous result? Their fitness must, on any

theory, have been there 'ab initio'; and, since they are unchanging, the chemist of to-day can test their qualities. Hydrogen preserves its identity, whether blazing in the sun, or signifying its presence in the spectrum of Sirius, or buried in a coal-seam, or when just caught in the test-tube of the chemist: much the same is true of all the elements. Does the experimentor trace, in his crucible or retort, any spark of intelligence or forecast in any one of them? Or can the physicist detect a psychic trait in any physical energy whatever which may have had to do with the outfit and mission of the elements? Yet without the aid of marvellous intelligence, I contend that the inauguration of the elements, such as we find them to be, was impossible, and their career doomed to confusion and disaster.

M. You are still harping on that wretched 'design' argument. As I have shown, it was battered to pieces long ago by evolution. What have you been about for the last thirty years?

E. Amongst other things, trying to find intelligence in matter and physical energy, and

I have not succeeded : trying to do without, and again I have not succeeded. No doubt, as you say, it is the ancient fire-mist, with its remaining nucleus, the sun, which drives the steam-engine of to-day, and has supplied material and building-power as well as a motor, but without the intelligence of man there would have been no steam-engine. Throughout its history, man has used and controlled an energy which is physical, and a matter which is inert. When I can believe that the intelligence of Stephenson and his predecessors had nothing to do with that superb machine—that all has come from the accidental observance of the lifting of the lid of a boiling pot, and a certain lucky environment of that fact, at the time and since—then I may also believe that intelligence has played no part in that amazing complex of phenomena which we can clearly discern, even from such little peep-hole as we are limited to.

M. Intelligence, in a sense, no doubt there was. Original matter must of course, according to my view, contain the potentiality of all things, and therefore of mind and intelligence.

E. But your 'potentiality' is not enough. 'In posse' will not do: 'in esse,' and that in a most active shape, is required from the beginning: we cannot wait for that long subsequent date when intelligence, as the accompaniment of animal life and mind, is to make its first appearance. We have questioned these late-comers before, and a few words must now suffice.

Take **life,** vegetal or animal. As we have seen, science has decided that life always proceeds from previous life, and is never found save in association with the physical basis which we call protoplasm. Where to find the first protoplasm ? Chemic synthesis does not furnish it. No chemist has yet produced it, nor, so far as we know, does it ever appear even in nature's laboratory except under the influence of existing life. Life is first, protoplasm second: given life, then as much protoplasm from inorganic matter as you please. Your fact from the sheep-field counts for nothing: the grass, being alive, can of

course transmute whatever inorganic material
it requires.   Your embryonic fact is just as
useless.   The human ovum would still be a
wonderful bit of protoplasm if it had produced
nothing better than you and me ; but it had
a father and a grandfather and an ancestry
reaching back probably to a Simian ovum, and
from that possibly to a primal cell.   Find that
primal cell, and your discovery will be worth
something.   The performances and possibilities
of the human ovum sink into insignificance
when compared with the charges which burden
the primal cell ; for it is pregnant with the
future of all animated nature, and parent
of all cells to the end of time.   Another
of your facts, viz., that 'matter undeniably
did, at some remote period, pass from a non-
living to a living condition,' is equally true
and equally irrelevant.   No one disputes it
and no one can explain it.   'Spontaneous
generation' has been laughed out of court.
No 'differentiation of atoms,' nor 'automatic synthesis,' 'whereby some should
become alive,' will suffice : either alternative

is merely a pompous begging of the question.
Lord Kelvin's whim—the arrival of germs on
a meteorite—might serve our earth, if the
germs did not get burnt in transit; but we
should still have to find out how the meteorite
came by them.

Can physical energy in any form originate
life? You have advanced no proof of it. It
is quite true, as you say, that all the life on
our globe is dependent on the energy emanating from the sun, but no one pretends that
this energy originates organisms, however
essential it be to their maintenance and
spread. If wholly withdrawn, universal death
would no doubt follow : but sunlight, in certain directions at least, destroys germs instead
of creating them; and sun-heat, if too nearly
approached, makes short work of that protoplasmic basis without which life cannot be.
The natural heat of the human body is about
$98\frac{1}{2}°$: raise it for a short time by one-tenth,
and life ceases. Potential energy, in the shape
of food, is of course essential to life, and as
necessary to cerebration and muscular con-

traction as to nutrition. Energy may, in a
thousand ways, aid in the work of that unstable
and intricate animated machine which we call
an organism ; but, so far as we know, it cannot originate the machine, and whilst this is
going, life is master and controls all contribu-
·tory energy. Take physical energy in any
form—as motion, or in any of its thermal,
electric, or chemic modifications—in none of
these, and in no combination of them, has it
hitherto been proved capable of transforming
non-living matter into living. We shall
presently find a better use for evolution, but
try it just now as what you conceive it to be,
viz., a form of physical energy. In such
capacity, it can no more originate a germ than
the whirling of a mass of rock can, and a
germ there must be before there can be any
biologic outcome. Science may some day
show that parentless organisms can and do
spring up in energised matter, and the demon-
stration will be very welcome, but until it has
been made, we have no right to regard a non-
animate energy as the author of life.

Then as to **mind.** The only mind you admit is *protoplasmic.* So far as concerns animal intelligence—say of ant, dog, or man— you are correct enough. The biologist demands a protoplasmic basis, whether he looks on ' neurosis ' and 'psychosis' as two (Huxley), or as one under two aspects (Lloyd Morgan). Talk to him of potential mind in a fire-mist and he will laugh at you. An oak in an acorn, or a man in an ovum-cell, as often as you please : if also chemist and æsthetic, he will grant you potentiality of diamond in a lump of carbon, or of hydrochloric acid in H and Cl if they join hands, but hardly potentiality of a statue in a block of marble without a sculptor, and as for latent life and mind (they go together) in the fiery furnace of a sun—no, Sir.

Remember also the late date and inadequacy of the protoplasmic mind. It is tardy in appearing, humble in commencement, slow in unfolding. Roll into one all of it which has ever existed, unite every spark of intelligence which has shown itself in man or brute or cell since time began, and the total will not serve

for the undertaking with which intelligence
was charged from the beginning. Much less
those faint stirrings of sensation, perception,
and volition which are all there is to show for
ages.

You speak of this protoplasmic mind as
though it were the only instance of intelligence
which nature presents. I maintain that before
protoplasm, and outside of it, we have, in the
orderly harmony and endless adaptations of
inorganic matter, abundant evidence of the
operation of intelligence ; and further, that the
protoplasmic mind itself is but the exquisite
and crowning proof of such operation.

Evolution has to take us all the way from
'protyle' to the grey cortex of the thinking
human brain. The first half of the journey—
from primal matter to the humblest speck of
living protoplasm—is arduous enough ; the
second half is at least equally difficult. If a
superintending intelligence were indispensable
in the early evolution of inorganic matter, it
would seem even more necessary for the
inception and development of the wonders of

biology. We cannot now go into these again, but I, for one, entirely decline to admit that protoplasm—supposing it started, and backed solely by physical energy—could find its own way, from the protozoan cell up through the interminable ascent of the animal series, until it burst forth in the splendour of a Plato, a Newton, or a Darwin.

In examining energy we have had, as one of our guides, the late Prof. Balfour Stewart. In the last edition (1890, lately re-issued) of his book, "The Conservation of Energy," at pages 78 to 82 he enumerates eight Forms of Energy; but neither in this list, nor in subsequent description, is there a word of any psychic variety, nor of an indwelling intelligence in any form of energy, as defined by science. Most physicists agree with Balfour Stewart. Add, if you like, the 'Röntgen X-rays,' but you will not be helped; they fall under "Radiant energy."

Thus, except as a dream, or as an item in a creed, there can be no more claim to psychism for energy than there is for matter. Science,

awake and sober, pronounces matter to be
inert and energy to be physical. Therefore
there is in them no source nor provision for
that initial intelligence which is indispensable,
nor yet for the faint copy of it which biology
finds later on. Up to the present, we have
had two factors—matter and energy. I now
claim admission for a third, viz., an adequate
and controlling intelligence. You say this is
present, from the beginning, in energised
matter. Science says it is not. No biologist
will admit the potentiality of mind in the
absence of protoplasm. The day of 'mind-
stuff,' unless the stuff be protoplasmic, has
gone by.

Either then you must accept my factor, or
enlarge your notion of energy. If you adopt
the latter course, you will have to seek inspi-
ration elsewhere than in motion of matter, and
cease importuning science for what she cannot
give. Better accept my alternative, and let
energy remain what science declares it to be,
viz., physical. But a source of life and mind
we must none the less have ; and, even if we

entrust energised matter with the business, in
the course of ages, of producing life, we cannot
extract from it an intelligence which must be
present long before life begins. If you reject
both my suggestions, your hypothesis has to
go a-borrowing for intelligence. Where to?
Under your conditions, no biologist will hear
of 'potentiality.' Where else? Surely you
will not stoop to a loan from eastern Pantheism,
or make shift with such a superstition as a
diffused 'anima mundi'? You, who are so
scientific.

Let us now see whether there be not some
better conception of evolution than that which
degrades it into a mere variety of physical
energy. You have called it, most appro-
priately, a 'master-key.' Possibly we have
overlooked some storehouse of help which it
can unlock.

CHAPTER II.

IS EVOLUTION POWER,
OR MANDATE?

*"A prima descendit origine mundi Causarum
series."*

E. ALL the world now recognises the great
importance and value of the hypothesis which
Darwin and Wallace were amongst the first to
seize upon and work out, and which has been
so luminously expanded by Spencer.   Applied
at first to the problems of animal and plant
life, evolution is now held to explain the course
of inorganic nature also, back to its earliest
period.   In its application to man, it is called
on to interpret not only his physical history,
but all his mental and moral progress, all his
social, ethical, and even religious advancement,
down to the days we live in.   Thus, according
to its extreme adherents, evolution is the key
to most of the enigmas of the universe.   It
explains the advance of matter from physical

uniformity to aggregation, from chemic homogeneity to elemental diversity, and from these,
step by step, until the whole of inorganic
nature is accounted for.   Then, when once the
leap to life is taken (and evolution, according
to some, reveals even this), the work is half
accomplished, and the ascent from the primal
cell to man becomes only a question of time.

Most of this can I think be accepted, if the
real nature of evolution be borne in mind.
For me, evolution is an instrument of research,
a ' master-key ' if you like, or a law, a plan, a
process, a mode of procedure, an explanation,
a history : not in any true sense, a POWER.
Behind it, and causing it, at every step, is
that intelligent force which, under different
names and differently localised, we both admit.
Without this force, evolution could not stir.
If you choose to regard evolution as in itself a
constituent part of energy, I am ready to give
it rank, ' pro tanto,' as a power.   But then it
is wasted, being merged in a force which we
have already assumed to be ample.   Its characteristic value is gone, and we cannot afford
such a loss.   The better way is, whilst

maintaining the natural distinction between evolution and energy, to ascertain so far as we can the important relations which exist between them. In attempting to show more in detail the significance of evolution and its relation to energy, I shall use the ground common to both of us, viz., that, somehow and somewhere, force and intelligence are in co-operation; matter of course is taken as present, and I may have a word to say on the relation, if any there be, between evolution and matter apart from energy.

The mere evolutionist seems to me like a man who cannot see the wood because of the trees. He buries himself in a mass of details, patiently adds link to link in his unending chain of facts, shows how each minute circumstance entails, or is caused by, or is otherwise related to, its surroundings— how, in his own language, each fact and circumstance influences, and is influenced by, its environment—until he loses his way in the maze, or struggles out with the end of a trailing chain in his hand, having found nothing to fasten it to. His wiser brother says this will not do. The human mind will not rest until this chain or network of fact and circumstance (phenomenon and environment, if you prefer the terms), be it ever so long, widespread, and intricate, is firmly attached to something which will hold it; and this Something—be it matter, or energy, or intelligence, or any combination of the three, or a Noumenon behind the three—stands ultimately in the relation of origin or cause to all phenomena.

I am aware that, of late and in certain quarters, the necessity for this ' something ' has been disputed : but the contention amounts virtually to a reopening of that old and obsolete question, whether chance has, or has not, ruled the universe. For ourselves, we have settled this point, and evolutionists certainly cannot regard the question as an open one, for they are perpetually confronted by causal relation : amongst them, in English-speaking countries at least, their philosophic chief, Mr. Spencer, is ' facile princeps,' and he traces all phenomena back to a supreme, persistent energy.

Those who deprecate the idea of causation

condemn it chiefly on the ground that it is a
mere expedient, a bit of guess-work, invented
by the human brain to bring some sort of
order and harmony into its own inchoate conceptions. They contend that all we have
before us is the interaction of a multitude of
phenomena which may precede, coincide with,
or follow each other, as the case may be, or may
appear to us as doing so : that ' causation,'
applied to elucidate all this, is a figment of
the imagination, unnecessary, unproven and
proving nothing, serving mainly as an illustration of the way in which the human mind
contrives to solace its insatiable curiosity. As,
however, this same mind happens to be the
only instrument we possess, I, for one, am content to abide by what seem to be its legitimate
methods and conclusions. We habitually
recognise causation in practical, everyday life,
and rely upon it as a reality : to admit it in an
exercise of thought is at least equally reasonable.
It is useless to attempt to abolish the distinction
between sequence and con-sequence. Why
one sequence, and that constant, rather than

any of a thousand possible sequences, if one
and all are haphazard? Precedence, coinci-
dence, and sequence involve relation in time
and space, but they do not necessarily imply
or provide for interaction; yet this is equally
evident: there really are such things as cause
and effect, and mere precedence can never
stand for the one, nor mere sequence for the
other. If instead of causation, we speak of
' connected sequence,' or of ' collateral relation,' we do not thereby get rid of that old
notion of cause and effect which has served
the plain man so long and so well. We are
only re-clothing it in more fashionable words;
and if causation is to be relegated to the limbo
of discarded fancies, I am afraid the credit of
evolution will also suffer. The chief function
of evolution is certainly not a bare cataloguing
of precedence, juxtaposition, and sequence,
amongst the facts and circumstances it pro-
fesses to explain. If this were all or principal,
the extraordinary value of evolution would be
hard to prove; for any old-fashioned naturalist
of pre-Darwinian days could, if possessed of

sufficient information, draw up such a record.
But we expect much more than this from
evolution, and we are not disappointed. It is
essentially a delineator of the constant and
progressive interaction of phenomena, and is
engaged, not only in tracing out the relations
between objects and their environments, but
also in ascertaining what it is which determines
these relations, *i. e.*, what causes them. Its
business is, not merely to marshal facts and circumstances in their proper order and sequence,
but to show how this order and sequence are
set agoing and maintained—in other words,
what produces them. Thus evolution is perpetually occupied with causation: both are
indispensable, and may be rightly regarded
as allies and complementary of each other.

Let us now see what inevitably happens
when evolution comes to be applied. Groups
of interlinked facts, strings of related circumstances, causes and effects of all sorts and
sizes, are perpetually cropping up in the path
of the evolutionist; and, unless he is prepared
to see his work lost in confusion, he must

perforce classify these things, trace them back,
and arrange them in the order of their date,
importance, relation to, and influence on, each
other. In this process, multiplicity gradually
gives way to unity, and diverseness to sim-
plicity: types become less and less complex,
and fewer in number: the relation between
objects and environments grows simpler:
secondary causes disappear, absorbed by more
important ones, and these in their turn
diminish in number and become unified.
When this stage is reached, the evolutionist,
if he be a genuine agnostic, will throw up his
clues, declaring they run out into utter
darkness: then he will settle down behind
his veil of sense-impressions, content with the
phenomena which reach him. But, if reso-
lutely bent on completing his enquiry, he
may decline to find a goal, whether in
unresolved phenomena however simplified,
or in a supposed impenetrable barrier beyond
them ; then, he is driven to trace on to some
sort of primal or originating cause. Many
scientists, as well as philosophers, insist on a

'noumenon' behind every phenomenon, and
infer its existence as they infer the existence
of anything whatever outside their own consciousness.   The 'noumenon' may be what lies
behind the small group of phenomena which
we have agreed to call a table or a man : or
it may be the great, universal Noumenon,
which Mr. Spencer calls " persistent energy,"
and which stands behind the phenomena of
the universe.   This may well be ' unknowable,'
in the sense of incomprehensible, inscrutable ;
but, since we, know (*i. e.* infer) its existence,
and know (also by inference) that the
phenomena of the universe are manifestations
of this ' unknowable,' we can scarcely be said
to be in complete ignorance.   As scientists
tell us, we are in precisely the same predicament with respect to matter, *i. e.*, we know
(infer) its existence from certain phenomena.
An anthropic mode of knowledge, no doubt,
but our only one and therefore valuable.   To
find the completely ' unknowing ' animal, we
have to descend below the human level.   We
shall seek it in vain in that intellectual caste

which has adopted the cognomen of 'Agnostic.'
An ox is a perfect agnostic, a man is not, and
can not be. (Our means and mode of knowledge are more fully discussed in the next
chapter.)

When evolution has thus carried us back to
the question of a primal cause, its office as
guide and interpreter comes to an end. It
has ushered us into the presence of a final
scientific trinity—matter, energy, and intelligence—then its function ceases. It cannot
evolve matter out of nothing, nor yet energy ;
as to their origin, it is utterly dumb ; with
regard to intelligence, it is equally helpless.
The mocking agnostic has halted at a lazy
spot in the rear called ' ignoramus,' evolution
has ceased to speak, and we are left to choose
for ourselves. We might select a spontaneous
generation, ' ex nihilo,' of matter, energy, and
intelligence, if it were not so absurd ; or adopt
your idea of an eternal, intelligent, energised
' materies,' if science would ratify it. We
may rest content with phenomena, or find
their ' noumenon ' in a persisting triumvirate

of matter, energy, and intelligence. Or, like
you, we may choose a single inclusive cause,
though a different one, as is done by Spencer
and the monotheist. The comparative reason-
ableness of these alternatives must be settled
by each thinker for himself, but once in face
of them, evolution can give him no further
help. Unless, indeed, those are right who
hold that evolution is even yet not quite silent,
but pointing distinctly to one single origin,
whether of matter, energy, or intelligence.

There is a side issue which we must notice
in passing. The attempt has sometimes been
made to discover, by a minimising expedient,
some other adjustment of matter, energy, and
evolution. A drop of water, a grain of silica,
an atom of oxygen, a microscopic cell, seems
to need so small a dose of energy and to
imply so trivial a movement in evolution.
With gradations so minute, circumstances so
trifling, progress from one step to another so
imperceptible, one requires only an infinitesimal energy for each infinitesimal step, and
the process of evolution, once started, may

surely be left to work of itself over distances
so insignificant.   No such belittling can,
however, affect the question.   The microscope
is balanced by the telescope, and the problem
remains the same whether for suns or pebbles,
for man or amœba.   If energy be served out
in driblets to every atom in the universe, it is
simply distributed, not lessened, and its
relation to evolution is unchanged.   Nor does
time make any difference.   Every *when*
preserves its relation to energy as accurately
as does every *what* and *where*, and the
attitude of energy to evolution remains the
same.   Energy does not alter its character
whether operating on a thimbleful of sand or
a solar system, during an æon or a moment :
and if evolution be not automatic for a man,
neither is it for an epithelium-cell.

M. Your rhetoric is running away with
you.   I have no wish to depreciate energy,
nor yet to disturb the harmony between
it and evolution.   Have I not throughout
insisted that the energy in matter is adapted
to every emergency it has to encounter ?

E. Undoubtedly ; and in exploring this
by-path, I have only wished to show that,
whilst no subdivision nor distribution of
energy can alter its import, so also the
relation of evolution to energy remains exactly
the same, in the smallest as in the largest
instance. Resuming my argument, I contend
that evolution can neither orginate nor include
the self-development faculty you attribute
to matter.   It will exhibit, in the clearest
manner, how energy has been applied in the
development of matter, but not why it should
have been so applied ; it can show, even be,
the way; it cannot explain why the way is there.
Evolution is ' modus,' energy is ' potentia ' ;
the control of both rests with ' mens.'

Evolution is equally at fault when applied
to matter.   It can tell us nothing of the
origin of matter, nor how matter came by the
properties which science assigns to it.   Only
when matter with its endowments, and energy
with its forces, are in the field, can evolution
put in an appearance.   Again, try your
master-key on that intelligence which we both

contend for, though we lodge it and appreciate
it so differently. Here surely evolution is
humble servitor. How can 'modus operandi'
possibly produce, or be also operator, and
find him brains into the bargain ? The idea
is absurd : the cart does not drag the horse,
nor is either of them driver, and if the act of
driving (evolution) takes place, a driver there
must be. 'Modus' is necessarily subordinate,
and dependent on some thing or power or
being which determines it. Evolution is
itself a thing to be accounted for, and needs a
cause.

Let us take the only occasion on which
evolution can be thought of as an originator
or creator, viz., the first appearance of life and
mind amidst inanimate nature. You, at any
rate, can admit no such claim, for you contend
that the potentiality of life and mind is
original in energised matter, and therefore
not *initiated* at any subsequent stage. Life
and mind may *appear* (as hydrogen and
oxygen may appear) at any date, and become
linked with an organism, but their poten-

tiality—*i. e.*, their latent presence, and the
power which determines their ultimate appearance—was there, according to you, from
the beginning and before evolution came into
play ; on your theory, whilst primal matter
was still uniform and homogeneous.   You
have called this appearance of life and mind
' a mere detail of evolution.'   That is true
though contemptuous.   Such a ' detail ' as
the passage from non-living to living is an
important one, and as yet enshrouded in darkness.   We are all hoping for the moment
when some inspired evolutionist shall succeed
in lifting the veil, but the significance of
evolution will not thereby be altered.   It will
still be interpreter, not cause.   The cause
lies long away back ; on your own showing,
ages before it came into visible operation in
the process which we call evolution.

Admirable, then, as an expositor, evolution
may unroll the story of the universe from
beginning to end ; it cannot evolve the forces
on which the universe depends, nor can it
ever include, eliminate, or explain away the

intelligent power which stands behind the
process. If we liken the universe to a
mighty river, evolution can mark out its bed
and banks and course; it cannot account for
the flood, nor for the force which impels the
flood. If we compare the march of the
universe to a stately history, evolution tells a
graphic story, but does not create the actors
and events.

Here seems to lie the great defect in the
explanatory value of evolution, so far as your
views are concerned. It cannot prove the
correctness of your fourth proposition[1], viz.,
that 'matter possesses inbeing power of self-
development.' If this power be otherwise
proven, or taken for granted, then evolution
will be a faithful servant. But it is quite
impartial: just as willing to serve the creedless
scientist who declines to deify matter, tracing
it and everything back to a persistent,
unknowable force; or the theist, who also has
his one sole cause of all: it will even serve
the agnostic, so far as he can make up his

[1] In Essay, from which these pages are taken.

mind to go. When once evolution has led
its votaries into the pantheon of the Gods,
they must choose a deity for themselves. It
will scarcely recommend 'Nihil,' supposing
that shadowy god to be there; nor is it
partial to a Syndicate of matter, energy, and
intelligence, but it will submit to that if needs
be; it would have served even the 'unknown
god' of the Athenians, if those old gossips
could have guaranteed his existence. Its
preference is distinctly for unity. If you or
the Monist can succeed in crowning matter,
it will yield allegiance, but it is at least equally
ready to bow before the Ultimate Cause[1] of
Spencer, or the 'Θεός' of the opponent you
most dislike. Materialism has no monopoly
of its services.

I have spoken of a great gap in the
explanatory value of evolution, and am sorry
to utter one depreciatory word ; but this
gap does not occur until a perverted and
forced use of evolution is attempted. As an
instrument of research it is invaluable, and
has about it the true scientific ring. Like the

[1] See Quotation, page 170.

first Law of Motion, it answers to 'how,' not
to 'whence' or 'why.' Newton does not
attempt to tell what matter and force are, nor
whence they sprang; but matter and force
being there, he shows us the 'modus' of what
has taken place, and will take place, between
them. So with evolution. It cannot tell us
what matter, energy, and intelligence are, nor
whence they came; but once there, it shows
their method of action. If we draw a com-
parison between this celebrated law of
Newton's and Evolution, and without dis-
paragement of the latter, this is surely adequate
eulogium. The one has stood the test of
scientific scrutiny for 200 years; the other,
in its Darwinian form, is not half a century
old, and though it has come to stay, it is not
yet quite a perfect guide. But its nature is
ascertained: it is mandate, not power. It can
account neither for 'materies,' 'potentia,' nor
'mens': its task is to register the method
and results of their co-operation.

In the Western thought of our day, the
materialist has two chief competitors, the

monotheist and the agnostic. Science, free
to all, is creedless. So also is the true
agnostic. His position is the 'Ignoramus
et Ignorabimus' of Emil Du Bois Reymond,
and is logical. But when he deviates
into materialism or spencerism, he becomes
a hybrid; greatly improved, no doubt, if
he follows Spencer. On the other hand,
materialist and monotheist are creed-holders.
The former has matter and physical energy
for his gods, eked out latterly by a hazy
'world-spirit,' or by dubious 'potentialities.'
When he attempts to press science into the
service of his creed, he finds Galileo as
recalcitrant as ever. Rather than a deification
of matter, many will prefer an apotheosis of
mind, and, with Newton, Faraday, and
Spencer, one supreme and undivided source
for all the phenomena of matter, energy, and
intelligence which the universe has to show.

*　　*　　*　　*　　*

In the next chapter, whilst aiming at the
same goal, we propose to try an entirely
different route.

Figure 1 (Reflex action).

Nerve-centre (**Nc**), formed by group of cells.
Nerve-fibres, passing to or from Centre.

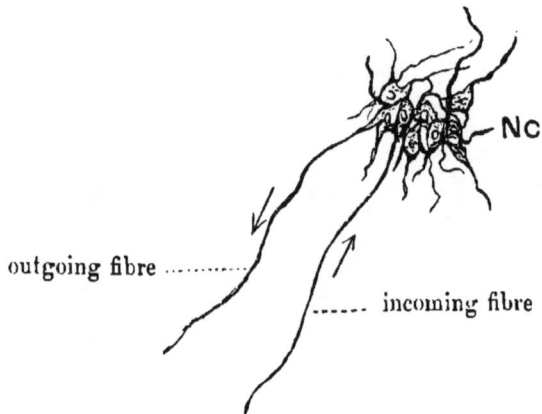

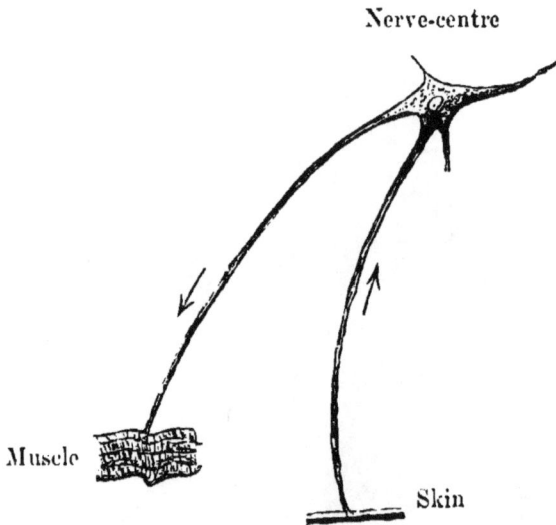

Nc

outgoing fibre ·············

·········· incoming fibre

Nerve-centre

Muscle

Skin

[After Schofield.]

CHAPTER III.

KINETICS AND METAKINETICS OF A BRAIN-CELL.

" Longum iter est per praecepta, breve et efficax per exempla."

POSSIBLY, even probably, any attempt to indicate mental processes by diagram will be considered fanciful and useless. We venture, nevertheless, to introduce a few figures, and in these two colours are employed —*black,* to signify what is held to be external and objective ; *red,* for what is subjective and psychic. We shall have to borrow some simple data from biology and psychology, and we commence by citing one or two in reflex nerve-action.

1. REFLEX INNERVATION.

Figure 1 represents the nerve-apparatus of

E

reflex innervation, reduced to its simplest
expression. It consists of a nerve-centre or
area, formed by one nerve-cell or a group of
cells, into which one or more nerve-fibres
(centripetal or afferent) enter, and from which
one or more fibres (centrifugal or efferent)
depart. At their inner ends, the fibres are
frequently continuous with the cells, and may
be regarded as greatly elongated arms whereby direct communication is kept up between
the cells and the structures they control.
In other instances, the inner terminal of the
fibre is in close proximity to the cell, but is
not continuous with it; this arrangement has
possibly a distinct purpose, and does not
impair the completeness and security of the
circuit. The in- and out-routes are permanent,
and not interchangeable : along the incoming
track impressions pass to the nerve-centre,
and are there converted into, or give rise to,
impulses which depart by the outgoing track.
In true reflex innervation, the nerve-centre is
strictly non-conscious, and the whole process is
essentially automatic. The term 'automatic'

is here used in its popular sense, not with its physiological meaning.

This reflex nerve apparatus is perhaps the earliest, and certainly the most widely extended form of nerve-system which is met with in the animal kingdom. In the lower invertebrata, the simple type we have described is apparently the only one which exists, and even in the highest, the same form prevails. In the vertebrate kingdom, the nervous system rests throughout on a broad basis of reflex arrangements. The spinal cord with its bulbar expansion consists mainly of a pile of reflex centres, connected, by outgoing nerves, with every muscle in the body ; and, by incoming nerves, with every sensitive area, and with all organs of sense excepting, perhaps, the olfactory : moreover, what may be termed the domestic functions of the body, viz., the whole of that visceral activity on which the maintenance of an animal depends, is relegated, almost entirely, to the sway of reflex innervation.

In the higher mammalia, and apart from

that which remains dedicated to nutrition, reflex action becomes increasingly masked by the association and control of the brain proper, itself a complex mass of nerve-centres; also by the co-operation of a dawning consciousness and intelligence. In man, it has become so greatly overshadowed that it is no longer quite easy to pick out a perfectly pure and simple reflex, suitable for non-technical illustration. The difficulty is increased by the fact that the same nerve routes (out and in) are used, to a great extent, by nerve impulses which affect consciousness or rouse and express volition, and by such as never pass further than a regulative, but non-conscious, nerve centre. As instances of natural reflexes we may name coughing, sneezing, swallowing (in part), breathing (also in part), and certain daily indispensable functions of the body. The example we select is the momentary *closure of the eyelids* which is constantly taking place during waking hours. Of course we can close the

eyes whenever we wish, and we can fix our
attention on their winking whenever it occurs ;
but, as everyone knows, this act is continually
happening whether we will it and observe it,
or not. Its chief purpose is to keep the
surface of the eye clean and moist : it is a
pure reflex, the nerve-apparatus concerned in
it being a twig of the fifth nerve reporting to
a centre in the medulla, from which a motor
impulse is sent along a branch of the facial
to the circular muscle which closes the lids.
Involuntary winking serves also another purpose in the protection of the eye against a
sudden blow, as from a missile ; the action
is still reflex, but the optic (retina) takes the
place of the fifth nerve.

Bearing in mind the extreme importance
and range of reflex action, and that even the
highest members of the nervous system are
not exempt from its influence, we are not
surprised to find in many mental processes
a close analogy with what is reflex. Indeed
there are scientists who, taking reflex action

in its widest and most philosophic sense,
are disposed to include under its rule, not
only the physical acts necessary to life, but
also the psychism of consciousness, volition,
emotion, and cogitation. Every variety of
psychic activity is thus held to be due
to excitor impulses issuing from the higher
cerebral centres, which centres, again, have
been thrown into action either by freshly
incoming impressions, or by these in association with the accumulated and registered
impressions and conceptions of previous experience. In this way, all cerebration may
be looked on as reflex, and as an illustration
of the self-adjustment, *re* nervous system,
of an organism to its physical and psychic
environment. The view, however, is somewhat transcendental, and quite beyond our
present object, which is to note the likeness,
and also the difference, between a simple
non-conscious reflex, and that particular form
of nervo-psychic action we propose to examine.
The thesis we have to develop may be stated
thus :—

Figure **2.** (A. and B.).

A. (Consciousness).

at rest   in action

B. (Protoplasmic conscious nerve area).

at rest   in action

A sense-impression, arriving at a nerve-centre or area which is conscious, may give rise, not to an outgoing impulse ending, it may be, in muscular contraction, but to a change in consciousness which results in the formation or 'projection' of a conception.

The action is neuro-psychic, not neuro-muscular.

* * * * *

2. Conscious Nerve-area. Excitants. Sense-impressions, and their Perception.

Starting, now, from the one fact of which each, for himself, is perfectly certain and without proof, viz., **consciousness,** we are equally sure that this is always in one of two states—in repose (as during dreamless sleep), or in action. We represent consciousness by a *red circle*—regular when in repose, irregular when in action. See Figure 2, A.

Science teaches that consciousness, in man, is associated exclusively with a certain area of brain-protoplasm, in which molecular changes occur concomitantly with changes in consciousness. We may take the association and changes *dualistically*, as Huxley does, and speak of ' neuroses' (molecular states and changes), and 'psychoses' (states and changes of consciousness): or, with Lloyd Morgan, we may take them *monistically*, and speak of one substance having two aspects— external or objective ('kinesis'), for physical states and changes; internal or subjective ('metakinesis'), for states and changes in consciousness. Either view will serve us, and both lodge consciousness in brain protoplasm. We now draw another figure representing the protoplasmic conscious nerve-area, its molecular basis in *black*: see Figure 2, B. This nerve-area has been called, in previous pages, the **protoplasmic mind.**

Experience convinces us that consciousness is roused in more ways than one, but notably and constantly by influences from the external

world. In view of their action on consciousness we propose, in future, to call these
external influences, **Excitants.** Such excitants, when they impinge on the periphery
of the body, rouse the activity of the outer
terminals of certain adapted nerve-fibres,
producing in them what are termed **sense-
impressions.** These impressions pass
inwards along the fibres, and are communicated by their inner terminals to the protoplasm of the conscious nerve-area. They
may arrive singly or in groups. They are
neural only, and are concerned in sight,
hearing, smell, taste, and touch. Under touch,
we include not only the highly developed
sense as it exists, for instance, in the finger-
tips, but also that general sensitiveness which
is present in the whole of the skin-surface,
and, in a less marked form, throughout the
interior of the body : we also include what
is sometimes called ' muscular sense.'

When sense-impressions reach the conscious
nerve-area, they arouse its psychic activity
and are responded to by **perceptions** of

light, sound, contact, position, shape, size, colour, taste, odour, &c., according to the nature of the impression which has been communicated. See Figure 3.

Sense-impressions, and also the perceptions to which they give rise, are, for the most part, accurate and trustworthy. We must insist a little on this point because their validity has sometimes been questioned : lately by an eminent thinker and statesman (Mr. Balfour, in his valuable " Foundations of Belief"). No doubt we have, in infancy, to learn to see, hear, and touch correctly, just as we have to learn to talk and walk : it is equally certain that, throughout life, sense-impressions have to be carefully scrutinised and construed by reason. We have also to sift out and exclude a certain group of well-known fallacies due to imperfection, disorder, or fag of the nerve-apparatus : such are colour-blindness, double vision, 'subjective' sensations, illusions, hallucinations, and the like. Again, sense-impressions may be feeble, uncertain, or thwarted by surrounding con-

Figure **3.** (Object and Concept).

Line of excitants *(black continuous arrows)*
> passing from external objects *(black circles on left)* to periphery of body.

Line of sense-impressions *(black dotted arrows)*.

Responding perceptions *(red arrows)*
> projected in the reverse direction and to the site of the external objects, as Conceptions *(red circles)* of these objects. The red arrows and circles, of course, should lie *on* the black ones; they are slightly displaced for sake of clearness.

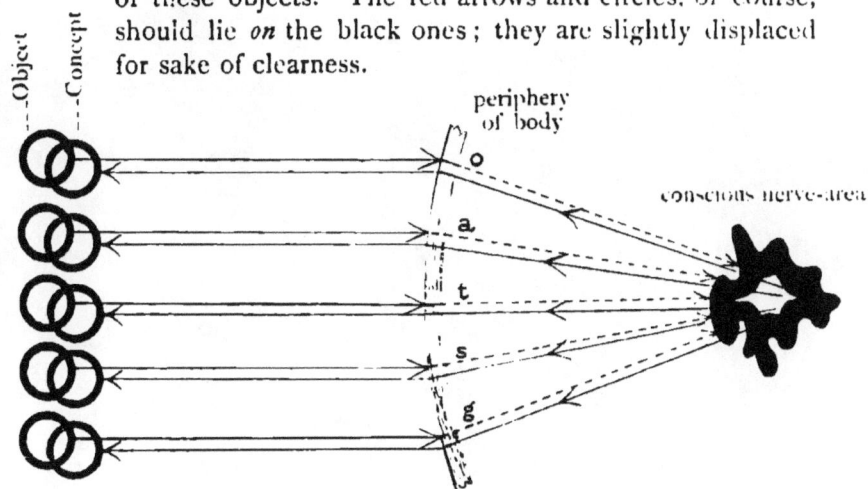

o. **optic**—for form, size, position, colour, movement.

a. **auditory**—for sound.

t. **touch**—for contact, resistance, weight, temperature, &c. ; also for form, size, position, movement.

s. **smell**—for odours.

g. **gustatory**—for taste.

ditions; they may be unheeded, or wrongly
interpreted ; they vary in intensity and
sharpness with the varying sensory acuteness
of each individual, with the attention and
amount of practice bestowed on them. Visual
impressions form the largest class, and it is
the trustworthiness of these which has been
most frequently called in question. No doubt,
as Helmholtz showed long ago, the human
eye is by no means an ideally perfect optical
instrument; yet, for the manifold usage of
life, it may be even better than a more perfect
organ. We do not put into the hands of
a soldier an exquisite rifle, which requires
delicate handling and a dust-proof and water-
proof cover, but one which will stand rough
treatment as well as shoot straight. There
are puzzles connected with vision which are
not fully cleared up, and perception of colours
is one of its curiosities; but no one, who has
an inkling of physiology, nowadays confuses
his visual perceptions of an external object
with qualities supposed to be resident in the
object. We shall presently have to examine

more closely the relation between object, excitant, sense-impression, and perception, but
just now our business is to vindicate the
character of sense-perceptions. When we say
a bush is green, we are of course speaking in
a conventional or convenient way. We do
not mean that green-ness is a quality of the
bush, but of the picture which, presented by
the optic nerve, is read-off green by perception. This reading is accurate, and as
it should be; otherwise how shall we distinguish between the bush and the gay
flowers which bedeck it, or secure that laugh
at the exceptional person who sees the bush
red? Instead of our perceptions of colour, in
its endless variety, being traps for the unwary,
they are rather proofs of the extreme exactness
with which the retina responds to probably
very slight differences in ether-vibration, and
of the equally wonderful fidelity with which
perception discriminates between minutely
differing reports from the optic nerve.

Language is steeped in metaphor and
imagery. We can hardly speak of an external

object without endowing it with some quality
or activity which we know it does not possess.
A bell *rings*, a shoe *pinches*, a knife *cuts*, a
door *creaks*, an engine *runs*, a pin (sometimes
a conscience) *pricks*, sugar is *sweet*, snow is
white and *cold*. It is scarcely fair, perhaps,
to say that our way of speaking of external
objects—as hard, smooth, soft, rough, red,
green, warm, cold, &c.—is merely meta-
phorical: it is really a remnant of ignorance
which we retain on account of its convenience,
and which the 'man in the street' still believes
in; but neither the scientist nor his critic
makes any blunder about it.

Our contention then is that, habitually,
our sense-impressions and the perceptions
founded on them are accurate and trustworthy. Were it not so we should indeed be
badly off, in view of the multitudes in which
they occur daily to everyone, and our utter
dependence on their guidance. Think for a
moment of the safety and success with which
they enable us to follow all sorts of mechanical trades and pursuits, many of them

requiring minute precision and involving risk
to life and limb. Think of the important part
which accurate sense-perception necessarily
plays in rigid and exact scientific work ; during
the recent eclipse, for example, or in the constant transit work of an observatory. Think
of the quick and true perceptions of a crack
shot, in covert, or in Indian jungle where his
life may depend on the correct planting of a
bullet in the right spot at the right moment ;
think of the keen-ness and accuracy of sight
and touch in the Wimbledon marksman, in the
Afridi 'sniper,' alas !, whose stolen rifle would
have been useless without his truth of vision
and touch. Remember the eye and hand of
an expert cricketer or billiard-player, of golfer
or tennis-player ; of the London bus-driver,
as he threads his difficult way through the
Strand at noon ; of the mariner, with one
sense fixed on the trembling needle and
another on the helm, as he steers a straight
course for the port he is making ; of the
surgeon in a delicate eye-operation, of the
artist at his easel, architect at his plans, en-

graver at his plate, watch-maker at his bench, ploughboy at his furrow, or even of the self-congratulating Irish hodman, precariously balanced on the rungs of a ricketty ladder, mounting bricks all day to " the other man at the top, faith, who does all the wurrk." Even our daily glance at the paper, or the writing of a letter, gives ample proof of the trustiness of average sight and touch. Try writing a few lines with the eyes shut : or try another sense altogether, and note the auditory perfection of the skilled conductor as he guides his orchestra though the intricacies of an overture ; listen to his first violin, or observe merely the musical precision of a clever piano-tuner. As a contrast to the reliance which experience has taught us may be placed on sense-evidence, note the helplessness of such as have been deprived of it. Watch a blind man in the street—how closely he listens, how painfully he gropes with his stick. Take away his hearing and his embarrassment is doubled : take from him also his sense of touch, and where is he ? The

three great classes of sense-impressions—
of sight, hearing, touch—are gone ; naught
remains but smell and taste, and these
blunted.   He is worse off than the man
struck down by coma, for he remains miser-
ably aware of the awful boycott which has
befallen him.   We are scarcely likely to
undervalue our sense-impressions or cease to
trust our perceptive interpretation of them,
seeing how faithfully we are served by both,
and how completely we are dependent on
them for any cognisance we can have of an
external world.

   We have been using two terms—sense-
impression, and sense-perception : for our
purpose, it is necessary to distinguish clearly
between these.   Sense-impression is *neural
only*, sense-perception is the psychic interpretation of a neural state : both are often
thought of, and talked about, much more
loosely than with the definite meaning we
attach to them.   A child is knocked down
and half-killed by a runaway cab ; it has had
very serious sense-impressions, but, being

instantly stunned, has scarcely perceived
them. Of the spectators, however, one has
what he calls an 'impression' that the driver
did not see the child, another has an 'impression' that the cabman shouted, another
that he was only swearing at his horse,
another that he was drunk, another that a
rein had broken, another is simply horror-
struck. They have all seen the accident from
about the same point of view, and have all
had practically the same sense-impressions,
but when they detail and compare their
supposed 'impressions,' it is not these, but
the product of them—the recollection, mental
picture, conception or judgment founded
thereon—which they recount.

We define 'sense-impression' as that
change which is wrought, on the nerve-tract
and molecular basis of the conscious nerve-
area, by the action of an excitant. We do
not need to determine what the change is;
it may be physical or chemical or electric, or
all three and more, or different from any—
science has not yet decided—but it is *neural*,

not psychic, and it is limited to the protoplasm of fibre and cell. The change, like the tract which it affects, lies intermediately between excitant and consciousness. It begins where the excitant rouses the outer terminal, or some other part, of the nerve-tract; it ceases when, at the inner terminal, it has aroused consciousness. Take, for example, the sense of hearing. Undulating air is the excitant; sense-impression is the change set up by this in the auditory nerve; perception of sound is the change in consciousness produced by the delivery of the sense-impression.

Thus when sense-impressions reach the conscious nerve-area, they produce, or result in, an active state of consciousness : *how, we know not.* Material and objective, in the nerve-fibre; material and objective even in the protoplasmic basis of the nerve-area, they nevertheless, in some unknown way, give rise to (are transmuted into ?) subjective psychic states. The first state produced is perception —the incoming impression is perceived ; but along with, or closely following perception,

there may be many states and changes.
Thus, together with perception may go a
feeling of pleasure, annoyance, or curiosity.
The incoming impression may be recognised,
or compared with predecessors, or silently
stored in memory. Or it may start a whole
train of mental pictures and processes: for
instance, an impression, incoming by the
olfactory route, may remind us of a certain
pleasant meal, of the scene, time of year,
friends present, where they are now and what
has since happened to them; and so may
lead on to volition, issuing in another dinner
invitation, or maybe in a cheque to an un-
lucky former guest who has come to grief at
the Antipodes.

There is, however, another way in which
incoming sense-impressions affect consciousness. They may lead to conceptions, or a
combination of conceptions, which are referred
directly to the external objects from which
the excitants, producing the impressions, are
supposed to proceed. Of such objects,
mental pictures or conceptions are thus

formed—are 'projected,' to use a word sometimes employed. The term is expressive, and
probably more accurate as regards visual and
tactual impressions; certainly it lends itself
more readily to diagrammatic presentation.

**It is to this last-named destiny of
sense-impressions that we limit our
enquiry, and we now proceed to examine a familiar and time-honoured
illustration of it.**

*　　*　　*　　*　　*

3. Orange, objective and conceptual.

Let an orange be so placed as to arouse
our sense-impressions. An excitant (say, an
ether-vibration of appropriate rate), reflected
from the surface of the orange, strikes the
outer terminal (retina) of the optic nerve,
produces therein a sense-impression which
travels inwards to the conscious nerve-area,
is there *re*ceived, *per*ceived, and gives rise
to (is transmuted into ?) a conception of
colour. But the retina, with its coverings, is

arranged as a camera and has lenses in front,
the result being that an upside-down image is
formed on the retinal terminal and constitutes
an important sense-impression : this is combined *en route* with a similar impression from
the other eye, the position of the reversed
image is rectified—we need not here enquire
how—and the result is that a corrected and
unified sense-impression is finally delivered at
the conscious nerve-area, and there gives rise
to conceptions of size, shape, and position.
These conceptions are checked and confirmed
by tactual impressions reaching the nerve-
area along nerves of touch. Such tactual
impressions of size, shape, and position are
perhaps truer than their corresponding visual
impressions, and may of course replace them,
as when the eyes are shut or blinded.[1] We

---

[1] In everyday life we trust largely to visual impressions because of their convenience, rapidity and
practical correctness; for distant objects, we have to
rely almost entirely on them, except where hearing or
smell are concerned. But there can be little doubt
about the aid which touch gives in the training of
sight; and in the appreciation of near objects, the two

have now only to add a sense-impression, travelling by the olfactory nerve and resulting in a perception of fragrance; and an impression arriving by the nerve of taste, resulting in a perception of sweetness and flavour, if the orange be a good one.

In reference to our orange, we have thus arrived at certain conceptions of shape, size, position, colour, fragrance, and taste. These conceptions are combined in consciousness, and 'projected' as a **conceptual orange.** See Figure 4.

Here comes a 'crux': the very one to nail a Naturalism-man on. The rustic says that what he is seeing, tasting, handling, is *the orange itself*, and he cannot be persuaded to the contrary. And all of us, in an ordinary way, speak of like-formed conceptions

---

senses remain in very close alliance. In all information afforded by the many varieties of contact (including the physical causes of pain, itching, tingling, &c.), touch is of course paramount. In certain cases, even for a distant object—for instance, a distant source of heat—it is touch, in a modified form, which comes into play.

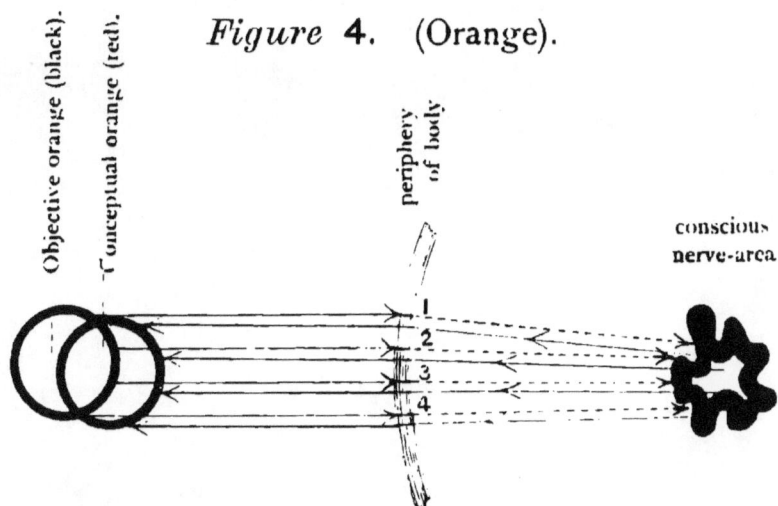

Figure **4.** (Orange).

Excitants *(black continuous arrows)*.

Sense-impressions *(black dotted arrows)*

Perceptions of sense-impressions *(red arrows)* combined and projected as Conceptual Orange.

1. (**Visual**) for colour, shape, size, position.

2. (**Tactual**) for contact, shape, size, position.

3. (**Olfactory**) for fragrance.

4. (**Gustatory**) for sweetness, flavour.

N.B.—As in Figure 3, the red arrows and circle should lie on the black ones; they are slightly displaced for sake of clearness.

of external objects as though they were the objects themselves. Science tells us we are mistaken in doing so, and must recognise the practice as a convenience only. All that we really perceive are the changing states of consciousness, and conceptions arising therefrom : out of these we construct conceptual oranges, tables, houses, &c. But, as we have seen, such changes in consciousness are brought about by incoming sense-impressions, and these again are produced by excitants external to ourselves. Even so-called 'subjective' sense-impressions are, as is well-known, produced by causes external to the conscious nerve-area. Thus a bit of diseased bone in the middle car may produce a sense-impression on the auditory nerve which is perceived in consciousness as a disagreeable sound, or a vascular disturbance in a blind retina may result in the perception of a luminous outline. Such starting-points within the body are, of course, as truly external to the conscious nerve-area as is a distant church-bell, or a star.

So far, in our observations, we have arrived at a definite result, viz., a conceptual orange. Tracing this back, we find it is the outcome of certain changes and conceptions in consciousness. These, again, are caused by incoming sense-impressions, which, in their turn, are produced by influences external to us. The series is thus:—

**External influence or excitant →
sense-impression → change in consciousness → conception.**

As we have seen, the plain man takes his conceptual for real: the scientist says he is wrong; what he is taking for reality is merely a combination of sense-impressions. The predicament is not avoided if we look on our orange simply as a mass of matter. Accomplished physicists assure us that we are entirely ignorant of what matter *is*, and must remain so. We can no more see and handle real matter than we can see and handle a real orange. Even Dr. Johnson did not touch reality when he kicked the stone with his philosophic toe. What we can know of matter is its properties, just as what we can know of an orange is its properties ; and such knowledge is obtained, in each instance, in the way indicated. Matter is held to be composed of molecules and atoms. But atoms and molecules are inventions of thought —conceptions of imagined entities which may, or may not exist ; 'ether' is a scientific conception or postulate ; the atomic theory and the corpuscular theory of matter are useful working hypotheses : that is all, and competent experts are not wanting who are prepared to clear them away, and substitute a hypothesis of 'units of force' for atoms of matter.

Bearing in mind this difficulty as to whether what goes by the name of 'matter' is a real entity or not, we return to our series as it at present stands, viz., **excitant ➡ sense-impression ➡ consciousness ➡ conception.** We should apologise for the apparent incongruity of thus linking objective with subjective, were it not clear that such association is constant in neuro-psychic action.

Of the series itself it may, however, be urged
that the only certainties are the last two
members. Whatever the excitant be, whatever modification it may undergo, wherever it
may come from and by whatever route, it (or
its modification) is delivered ultimately at the
innermost terminal, viz., the molecular protoplasm of the nerve-area, and is there as truly
external to consciousness as though it were
a hundred yards away; further, that of this
molecular protoplasm, or of any agitation
occurring in it, we can know nothing save in
the way of a conception. The monistic view
might here help, since it regards the molecular
agitation (neurosis) and the concomitant subjective activity (psychosis) as merely the
outside and inside aspect of the same thing.
But it renders no aid to that true and
complete agnosticism which says—' what I
know is consciousness ; all that I can know of
an outside world are the pictures and conceptions which arise in consciousness.' Anyone who seriously adopts this position is,
however, pretty certain to drift off, sooner or

later, into a world of phantoms in which the sole remaining certainty is his private consciousness, valid only for himself. Losing his grip of protoplasm, he has clutched a shadow; but this, too, eludes him. The " Ego cogito, ergo sum " of Descartes is really of no use to him. He is reduced to ' cogitare '—cannot keep even ' cogitans '—for he has begged his ' ego,' and we can take it from him. It is perfectly legitimate to call upon him to surrender it, for the introspective proprietorship, which this imaginary entity is supposed to possess, can quite readily be transferred to consciousness. We have only to regard consciousness as in part specialised to observe its own proceedings—as appliable and applied to itself—then the delusion of personality may be dismissed, a proprietor is no longer needed, and the ghost, if there be one, is left to cover its nakedness, if it have any, with such ownerless conceptions as may happen to be about.

From this dismal pitfall we are saved by the assured conviction of real existence which

every sane person has, and for which he asks
no proof. We may also remember, as
Professor Morgan reminds us (in "Monist,"
Oct. 1897), that each individual's experience,
whether correct or not, is, for himself,
undoubtedly real. The lad who, on a dark
night, has taken a flapping sheet of newspaper
blotted against the hedge for a ghost, and
has thereby been frightened out of his wits,
has had an experience very real and alarming,
though founded on false data. So also has
the well-meaning but over-worked signal-man,
whose tired eyes and weary metakinesis end,
at last, in the wrong lever and a fatal
crash.

* * * * *

4. Relation of excitant and sense-impression to consciousness. Brain-cells and Psychism.

With respect to the last two members of
our series—consciousness and conception—
we have thus no anxiety. Let us now see

whether an equal, or at least adequate, certainty can be established for the first two, viz., **excitant** and **sense-impression.** Fortunately they are open to very simple experiment.

Shut the eyes in broad daylight, and the sense-route (optic) falls at once into repose, no impression travels on it, and no perception of light occurs. Open the eyes, and an external excitant ([1] light) at once falls on the optic nerve, producing in it a sense-impression which passes on to the conscious nerve-area and occasions a perception of light. Control these observations by another. Open the eyes when in complete darkness, and no perception of light takes place. In the first and third instance—eyes shut in daylight, eyes open in darkness—two conditions are alike, viz., perceiving area and conveying

---

[1] We use the word 'light' in the ordinary way: more exactly, our excitant should perhaps be spoken of as that particular vibration of ether which is the proper stimulus of the optic nerve, and rouses its specific activity.

route ; there is capacity for sense-impression,
but the impression itself is absent, the third
necessary condition being either excluded or
not present. Introduce this condition, and a
perception of light at once follows. This third
condition concerns the first two members of
our series : with respect to them, and in so
far as the foregoing illustrations are concerned,
we draw two conclusions—first, that the
co-operation of excitant and sense-impression
is indispensable to the final result (seeing);
second, that both are external to, 'and
independent of consciousness, and of any
conception arising therein. The experiment
may be varied by shutting one eye whilst the
other is open, or by using a pair of eyes in
one of which the cornea is opaque or the
pupil blocked. A similar trial may be made
with any other nerve of sense. Take the
glosso-pharyngeal (nerve of taste) in a
quiescent state, the conscious nerve-area being
also quiescent so far as perception of taste is
concerned. Now bring to bear on the nerve
an external excitant from, say, a pinch of

salt or sugar; a sense-impression at once arises, and is presently followed by a perception of taste in consciousness. Again—touch gently the hand of one who is asleep: there is an excitant and a sense-impression, but both too feeble to rouse the slumbering consciousness : now squeeze the hand smartly, and consciousness awakes, possibly very cross. Let the sleeper be heavily drugged, as by chloroform, and nothing will rouse him : that terrible excitant, the surgeon's knife, and the violent sense-impression produced by cutting through sensitive nerves, are for the moment totally unheeded ; but consciousness will rage presently, when the merciful spell has passed.

Try yet another simple experiment. Take an insulated piece of copper wire, having a movable needle connected with one end of it ; at the other end introduce a current of electricity, and the needle is immediately deflected. In this case, the electric current represents the external excitant of our previous observations, the copper wire takes

the place of nerve-fibre, the change in the
particles of the wire produced by the passing
current represents sense-impressions, the
needle stands for the molecular protoplasm
of our nerve-area, and the movement of the
needle for ' neurosis ' or ' kinesis.' Let us
suppose, for a moment, that in the moving
needle there is an area of consciousness : in
this case, a subjective state ('psychosis' or
' metakinesis ') would at once arise, and result
in the conception or mental picture of a
moving needle.   There is no such area in the
needle, but we need not be at a loss, for it
is easy to switch on a human consciousness.
Let A, who is to supply the consciousness,
have his eyes bandaged and ears stopped, so
that no sight nor sound can reach him ; then
let another person, B, conduct the experiment.
It is complete and successful, but A, though
present, is none the wiser.   Continue the
experiment as before, but connect A's consciousness by removing bandage and stopping,
and   immediately A becomes aware of the
whole business.   In his consciousness he has

a perception of the moving needle; he can hear its click, or the ringing of a bell if the current have been arranged to ring a bell as well as move a needle; and if he touch needle or bell, he may get still another very direct and less agreeable proof of the reality and externalness of an excitant. To make sure, he may then perform the experiment on B. Of course we cannot connect the consciousness of A or B directly with needle or bell, nor even with the current; there is the inevitable loop-line of medium, eye, ear, skin, nerve-tract, and protoplasm of perceiving centre to be got over, but the connection is none the less effectually made in the end. Such experiments are sound and conclusive, for they can be repeated any number of times by any number of observers, and because the result is always the same and predictable with certainty.

By this time we are probably convinced that the excitants we have been experimenting with do veritably exist, do set up sense-impressions, and also that both are external to

consciousness and entirely independent of it.
So far from being to us merely conceptions,
we recognise in them causes and antecedents
without which no such conceptions would
arise. It may be objected that we can, and
often do form a mental picture or conception
of an external object when no such object is
present, and therefore no excitant and no
incoming sense-impression. The objection
seems valid, but is easily met. Such an
apparently non-caused conception has simply
been summoned from the storehouse of
memory. Originally produced by an incoming
sense-impression, it has been repeated,
refreshed, strengthened by a long succession
of such impressions, until it has become a
permanent and available mental asset, at the
service of either volition or association. Not
of course retainable without its protoplasmic
companion. We do not in the least know
what the companionship is, nor how long it
will last, nor how end, but in the present it
is indissoluble. The carriage and retention
(so to speak) of such conceptions imply, for

the biologist, the continuous existence of
appropriate brain-cells, and may, without
committing him to either dualism, monism,
or materialism, be fairly regarded as a function
or office performed by such cells. Brain-cells,
like all others, in their successive generations,
hand down type, structure, and function with
extreme fidelity. Thus it may well be that,
in recalling what appears to be a past conception, we are really dealing with a closely-
resemblant successor. If the metaphor can
be permitted, we may be merely reading,
not the original imprint, but a facsimile of
it, maintained in stereotype by succeeding
generations of brain-cells, and presented by
the generation actually existing.

There are still some who find, in the
memory of their past experience, a convincing
proof that personality and psychic states, re-
lating to the past, may exist without a physical
accompaniment, and be in some way independent of the brain. The protoplasm concerned in our past experience, say they, has
long been defunct, yet our memory of that

experience remains, and is at times uncomfortably vivid. Those who hold this view are of course forgetting the registering and bequeathing power of brain-cells ; and the theory of memory above given is certainly more in accord with the imperative dictum of modern biology, viz., that for every psychic state and event there is an associated presence of, and movement in, brain-protoplasm. The same theory also at once rids us of the difficulty in understanding how mental pictures may arise in consciousness, apparently in the absence of an external excitant. The constituents of the picture are already in the safe keeping of some morsel of brain-protoplasm, and nerve arrangements are provided whereby such constituents shall be produced when consciousness calls for them. Such a morsel (brain-cell) may be compared to a cell in the battery we were using. Let the nerve-battery (protoplasm of brain-cells) be thrown into action—it is quite at the mercy of its surroundings—and an excitant is at once forthcoming which may summon, and send along the prescribed route a stored impression, or its psychic equivalent, which presently makes its appearance in consciousness. As electricity may be stored, so undoubtedly may nerve-force, and an unnoticed trifle may set either free. Of the storage and routine application of nerve-force, at a stage in advance of what is simply reflex, we have a good illustration in that action of certain nerve-centres which physiologists call 'automatic.' It is exemplified in many acts which habitual repetition has at length rendered almost independent of volition; as instances may be cited the half-mechanical execution of familiar music, and the act of walking, continued perfectly though the walker has lost himself in thought. Between this kind of routine storage and usage of nerve-force, and that whereby mental energy is accumulated and applied in the commoner forms of psychic action, there is probably a close analogy.

At one time, dream conceptions, occurring when the senses are at rest in sleep, were occasionally quoted as instances of conceptions arising independently of sense-impressions. We now know, or think we know, that dreams

depend on the fact that consciousness, not
perfectly at rest, is open to the invasion of a
pack of acquired conceptions, set at liberty to
play high jinks, in consequence of the sus-
pended inhibition of a half-asleep brain, like a
parcel of schoolboys when the master is nod-
ding. We further know that many vivid
dreams owe their origin to the arrival of
actually fresh, though distorted, sense-impressions. Thus the frozen miner in Klondike
of our dream turns out to be a staid fellow in
London who has merely kicked the blankets
off; the sybarite, buried deep in a feather
bed, becomes Thomas Atkins, marching with
a heavy load on his shoulders over an endless
sand-waste under a blazing sun; an im-
prudent supper results in a grinning demon
on the pit of the stomach at 3 o'clock in the
morning, and unlimited whiskey leads to a
waking dream of 'blue devils'; &c., &c. In
disease, as is well known, morbid physical
conditions within the body give rise to innumerable disagreeable sensations and gloomy
forebodings in consciousness.

We have dwelt on these illustrations because it is important to establish beyond question the relation between external excitant, impression on nerve, and subjective conception. To those who are familiar with the subject, most of what has been written will be trite and superfluous, but to such as have no time for dabbling in biology and psychology, even a few elementary matters may be useful. Up to the point we have reached, our contention is that, in the great majority of instances, there is a causal sequence operating on a line passing from without inwards towards the conscious nerve-area, and whether the excitant arises outside or inside the brain. Further, that the disturbance of consciousness which results in conceptions of external objects can, as a rule, no more occur without the co-operation, direct or remote, of sense-impressions, than, in reflex innervation, a motor impulse can issue from a non-conscious nerve-centre unless preceded by an ingoing excitor impulse.

✳ ✳ ✳ ✳ ✳

5. Source of Excitants. Reality.

We have now to make a further short examination of the first member of our series, the **excitant,** and learn what we can of its *origin*. We take for granted that its existence, externalness, independence of consciousness, line of direction and route as regards the perceiving nerve-area, have been established by the foregoing experiments. Further, we are convinced that so real an influence (excitant) as that which has unquestionably led to the disturbing of consciousness must itself have a real source or origin; for we entirely decline to believe that it arises in nothing and comes from nowhere. 'Nihil,' as the source or producer of an excitant, can scarcely satisfy even the wild imagination of a half-crazy philosopher.

Once more and for the last time we describe a simple experiment, the excitants to be examined being light as before, and heat. We do not stop to enquire what light and heat are, nor how they are related to combustion of hydro-carbons or clash of molecules

or vibrations of ether, nor how one rate of
vibrations corresponds to radiant heat, another
to light, a third to electricity, nor how it
comes that these rates may replace each other.
We take light and heat, as in common parlance
—light and heat of sun, lamp, gas-flame, &c.—
and, without going into detail, we speak of the
sun, ignited lamp, or gas-flame as the source
of the light and heat in question. For convenience, the description of the experiment is
partly in dialogue.

It is a bright, hot day. *A*, a shrewd gas-
man, but knowing nothing about sense-
impressions, nerve-areas, excitants and the
like, is led into a perfectly dark room where
there are arrangements of which he is ignorant.
To him enters *B*, a scientist; he manipulates
a certain apparatus, and the room is at once
lighted up.

"Well Mester," says *A*, "yo've browt a
leet in; Aw doant knaw wot it is, but it's
behoind that theer screen."

Again darkness.

A. "Now yo've takken t'leet awaa, or putten
it aght."

Again there is light: *A* pushes the screen aside, finds a burning lamp, and exclaims "Theer's t'leet, Mester; ony foo-il can see that."

B. "Can he? Try again."

Once more darkness, followed by light.

A. "Yo've browt t'lamp back agean; an' if Aw thowt yo wor 'umbuggin' me, yo'd get it at yer 'e-ad sharp, an' mebbe larn summat fresh abaght it."

When the screen is moved, there is no lamp, but a gas-flame.

A. "Wot difference docs that mak? It's t'gas as does it; if yo'll stick yer finger agen it, yo'll knaw an' oal; an' if yo blaw it aght, as Aw did wunst when Aw wor a lad, yo'll knaw it's theer, oal t'sa-ame, by t'smell."

Another interval of darkness, followed by light.

A. "Yo've gotten another leet behoind t'screen. Mebbe it's a cannel this toime."

The screen is moved, and an incandescent electric lamp is found.

A. "Aw knaw oal abaght that too. Aw've

a brother fits them things up, an' yo can turn
off t'lectricity same as yo do t'gas."

Again darkness, succeeded by light. This
time there is nothing behind the screen, and
A is at a loss. Presently he notices that the
light is flashed from certain points, and on
examining these he finds a cunningly arranged
set of mirrors, by which the light is dispersed
in all directions. But he knows mirrors do
not produce light. There's that old cracked
looking-glass in his bedroom, before which he
has shaved himself on many a dark morning,
but he had to light the gas before he could
do it. So he seeks further, and at last finds
a gap in the wall through which a strong
beam of light is entering, and sees how it
passes from mirror to mirror and is scattered
through the room.

A. " Well it's just t'sunleet. Yo've letten
it in through that 'oile."

B. " How do you know that ? From where
you are, you cannot see the sun. As a matter
of fact, the light is coming from a piece of
burning stuff, called magnesium, which is

behind the wall.   Now put your hand opposite
this other hole, when I draw the slide back.
You feel a strong heat coming in, and if you
hold this bit of glass in its way and put your
pipe at a certain place before the glass, we
shall set the tobacco on fire.   Where do you
suppose the heat comes from?"

A. " Doant knaw ; mebbe yo've putten a
furniss behoind t'wall."

B. " No.   This time it is the sun.   We
have merely arranged a contrivance outside
for collecting its heat, and sending it through
the hole.   Come and look at it."

They go out into the sunshine.

B. " Now then, can you touch the sun?"

A. " No, but Aw can see it."

B. " Shut your eyes a moment.   Now
where's the sun?"

A. " It's theer oal t'toime, Mester.   Aw
can feel it."

B. " What without touching it?   But you
are right enough.   On a hot day like this,
we can feel better with our heads than our
hands, and that is why yon lady has her

parasol up. Go back to your gas a moment. It is leaking somewhere, and presently the room will be full of it. You can neither see it nor touch it, and if you had a bad cold in your head you might not smell it; but if some idiot were to bring a light in, we know what would happen. Do you think you could touch the sun, if your finger were long enough?"

A. "Mebbe Aw cud. But it 'ud happen get melted."

B. "I know a lady who has lately grown a tremendously long finger, which will not melt. It is ninetythree millions of miles long, and she can put it exactly in the place where the sun is; yet she cannot touch the sun, any more than you or I can. Strangely enough, she can feel its light, by the trembling of her finger : indeed the light will travel along her finger and reach the place where she is standing, 93 millions of miles off, in just about eight minutes. But her finger is far longer than that; she can stretch the tip of it to stars so distant that their

light takes scores of years to reach her.
She can even tell sometimes that the light
has broken off, and the stars gone out."

A. "Them's ta-els, Mester. Yo doant
expeck me to b'lieve 'em."

B. "I can introduce you to the lady, and
she will show you her finger, if she still has
it about her. Such things have a way of
dropping off. But 1 know she has it now."

A. "They saay seein's believin', but Aw
shouldn't b'lieve oal that, not if she wor to
show me twenty fingers."

B. "Well, you can make her acquaintance
any day. Her name is Science, and if you
will listen to her a while she will convince
you, as she has convinced me and many far
wiser than you or I will ever be, that all
we call touching, seeing, smelling and so on,
is done in a little spot inside our heads.
There we sit all day long and night too,
receiving and sending messages like a tele-
graph clerk in his office, but with this
difference—we have to sleep in the office,
and can never get out as long as we live."

A. "Aw've 'eerd summat loike that afore.

A chap once tell'd me 'e cud sit in 'is own 'e-ad, an' 'ear t'clock strike, an' see little picters; but Aw thowt 'e wor a bit luny. Look 'ere now, Mester. 'Ere's this bench we're settin' on. It's 'eavy an' it's 'ard cos it's med uv iron, an' it's pented green, an' it s got a se-at an' a back an' fower legs. Do yo me-an to tell me we're settin' on nowt, an' as 'ow Aw'm a jackass an' can't tell t'difference atween a picter in my 'e-ad an' this 'eer bench? Aw've a little lad as goes to school, an' a sharp little chap he is too ; whoy he'd mak yo a picter of t'bench in no toime, aye, an' pent it too; an' he'd knaw t'picter warn't t'bench, just sa-ame as yo an' me does."

B. "None the less, my friend, if you did not form a picture of it in your head you would not see the bench, and if your little boy did not do the same, he could not make his drawing. The picture does not stop in your head: without knowing it, you have planted it just where the bench is. But there is a real bench, and we are sitting on it, though we can neither see nor touch it."

A. "Aw wor sartin theer wor summat
'eavier nur a little picter."

B. "And you were right. You were
only wrong in the way you were trying
to prove you could see and touch the real
bench, or can see, touch, or smell the things
you are working amongst every day—gas,
pipes, gasometers, retorts, coal, &c. You are
dealing all the time with real things, though
not in the way you imagine. Have a chat
with the lady. She is everybody's friend,
and will tell you far more than I can. In
the end, she will convince you that you
can no more touch the real thing in a gas-
flame, not even though your fingers get
burnt, than you can touch the sun."

A. "Aw'll see her abaght that onyway,
Mester. Aw doant b'lieve as 'ow Aw'm
not touchin' t'fla-ame, wi' my fingers frizzlin'
in't. It 'ud be a merrycle."

Thus scientist and workman agree that
underlying every external object there is
reality, though workman is wrong in the
way he takes his sense-evidence. And

metaphysician agrees with both, unless he
be one of the rare sort whose sole reality
is consciousness, or one of the still rarer
kind who can accept 'nihil' as an origin
for excitants which are continually rousing
his consciousness. The man of science is
cast in a different mould. When he has
resolved heat, light, electricity, into vibration,
he immediately seeks about for what it is
which vibrates, and if he cannot find it, he
invents it : his scientific instinct compels
him to assume ether, as he did atoms. And
if, some day, he finally routs the 'units-of-
force' men, and demonstrates conclusively
the existence of ether and atoms, he will then
tell us they fall into the same category as
the workman's bench, and, equally with it,
demand a reality.

Science does not admit phenomena [1]
without noumena to account for them.

---

[1] In this 3rd chapter, the word '**phenomenon**' has
hitherto been purposely avoided, because it is used
in speaking both of what is objective and what is
subjective, and so is liable to produce confusion. As
antithetic to '**noumenon**,' it is in its place.

*　　*　　*　　*　　*

It would thus seem that we are now
entitled to complete our series by prefixing
a fifth member, viz., **reality**. In this case,
the series would be :—

Reality (noumenon) → **excitant** (phenomenon) → **sense-impression** → **consciousness** → **conception.**

If an objector says we have no right to
this new member except as a postulate or
assumption, we reply—Very good ; take it
at that, but take the consequences. The
evidence for the existence of anything whatever rests finally, for each individual, on
the testimony of his consciousness. He can
never leave his protoplasmic prison, and must
content himself with what can reach him
there. Science admits this, though she
insists, as we have seen, on the particular
way in which the testimony of consciousness
is elicited. We see and touch (as we say)
an external object, and are sure we are
dealing with a reality, though not in the
rustic's way ; but the ultimate evidence on

which this assurance rests is the testimony
of consciousness. It is this testimony alone
which, in the last resort, convinces us that
we have such things as arms and legs;
indeed, upon it alone, each one, for himself,
rests his unshakable conviction of so important and fundamental a matter as his
individual existence. We submit that, though
often criticised, the Cartesian aphorism,
' **Cogito, ergo sum,**' remains perfectly valid.
Cogito implies **cogitans,** thinking implies
thinker; just as motion implies something
which moves, just as vibration implies a
medium. Two hundred and fifty years of
cogitating, aided by a century and a half
of modern science, have altered, not what
is expressed, but the mode of expressing it.
Huxley insists quite as strongly that ' psychosis ' involves ' neurosis,' and Lloyd Morgan
that ' metakinesis ' implies ' kinesis,' as
Descartes insisted that thinking proves
thinker. The dress is modern, the wearer is
not. Even if we take its very latest fashion,
viz., " the indisputable axiom *Experientia est*"

(see " Monist " for Oct. 1897, page 4) of the
genial Bristol Professor whose guidance,
valued in the past, is a cherished hope for
the future, we do not seem to have advanced
much. We peep inside the robe, and there
is the very same dame, though a trifle older :
she has changed her name—it is a way ladies
have—from Cogitatio to Experientia, and
the later name perhaps better befits her
maturity. Otherwise she is wonderfully pre-
served. Something is 'experienced' which
was formerly 'thought'; somebody experi-
ences who formerly cogitated. We still have
to ask, whose experience?, as the French
philosopher asked, whose thinking?, and the
same reply answers both questions.

It suits our purpose exactly to find
'Experientia' (*née* 'Cogitatio') remaining so
vigorous, above all, so real ; and the ground,
cleared and occupied by Descartes 250 years
ago, stable and tenable as ever. But we
must remember that, as the assured conviction of personal existence which each
individual possesses rests solely on the

testimony of consciousness, so also does his
certainty that he has arms and legs, so also
his certainty about any external object.   If
he denies reality to sun, lamp, bench, orange,
&c., he is bound to deny it equally to limb,
eye, ear, nerve, and brain-protoplasm, since
all alike are external to consciousness : nay,
he must abandon his very existence ; it is no
longer real, and consciousness shrinks to a
bodiless phantom.   On the contrary, once
accept the testimony of consciousness as to
the reality of personal existence, and it may
be relied on equally for the reality of all
external objects, if sufficient and correct
evidence of them has been taken at the bar
of consciousness.   The battle for reality is
ultimately fought out in the brain-cells : if
it be won there, as many think it has been,
it is won everywhere.   We therefore submit
that the member now placed first in our
series is no mere postulate or assumption,
but a deduction as sound as the deduction
of personal existence from consciousness.
Further, that **reality**—be it assumed, postu-

lated, deduced, implied, or inferred—is
necessary to the very occurrence of consciousness: just as necessary as, for the
biologist, is that brain-cell protoplasm, which
all admit to be the nearest neighbour and
inseparable companion of consciousness, and
which, according to the monist, is incor-
porated with it.

*   *   *   *   *

6. REALITY. MEANING ATTACHED TO IT;
   RELATION TO MATTER AND ENERGY;
   EVIDENCE ON WHICH IT RESTS.

We are nearing our goal and have only to
add a few words about what is now the first
member of our series, viz., **reality.** Not
that we propose any metaphysical discussion
of what reality is. If in no other way, we
are warned off that dangerous ground by
the old Scotch professor—" when ae body
is tellin' anither body, wha doesna understaun' him, aboot maitters which he doesna
understaun' his-sel, that's metapheesicks."

So that, if asked what 'reality' is, we frankly say we do not know. That is, we do not know its *nature* : it does not follow that we know nothing at all about it, attach no meaning to it, and are wrong in looking on it as the source or origin of those external influences or excitants which affect consciousness. When Professor Tait says we do not know what matter *is*, and in all probability are incapable of knowing—that all we know of what is called 'matter' is a little of *structure*, and much (as his own admirable book shows) of *properties*—he quite recognises, unless our humble judgment is mistaken, that in or behind so-called matter there is a *something* (pass the term), intangible, invisible, and, in its nature, unknowable, because inaccessible to sense ; but still there, as **'causa vera,'** of all that bundle of properties which uninstructed people take to be matter itself, and which could not exist in the absence of this **'causa vera.'** This 'true cause' is what we mean by Reality, and is, like all true causes, independent of, and

prior to, its effect. We may call this effect
what we please—property, manifestation, phenomenon, influence, stimulus, excitant—but
it is entirely dependent on its predecessor,
Reality, though we can use it as proof of the
existence of that predecessor.

Conceivably, reality may be disconnected
from what is called matter; indeed, must be,
if energy or mental activity can exist apart
from material concomitants. As most people
are aware, matter is regarded as the "receptacle" or "vehicle" of energy. But let
us suppose, for a moment, that the association of energy and matter, at present held to
be inviolable, has been for some good scientific
reason discarded, atoms, ether, and corpuscular theory of matter banished, and a
theory of energy and 'units of force'
accepted in their place. What we now call
matter would then fall into line as a mode or
expression of energy. But reality would
remain : as indispensable to units of force as
to atoms of matter. Of the ultimate nature
of energy we know as little as of the ultimate

nature of matter, and experts alone can deal
with either question. But even lay-folk can
understand that such important forms of
energy as heat, light, and electricity are
modifications of motion, and that all forms of
physical energy are probably due to motion.
Layman, as well as scientist, is permitted to
enquire—motion of what?; and the answer
for either of them is, at present, motion of
matter. But when layman asks the man of
science what matter is, the reply he gets is
that we do not, and cannot know, and must
be content with a good working hypothesis
of material atoms and molecules; moreover,
since these are not supposed to occupy the
whole of inter-stellar or inter-planetary space,
and since action, without a medium, between
bodies at a distance is held to be impossible,
we are further compelled to postulate such a
medium, the one which answers our require-
ments best being 'ether.' If layman then
says—all we thus seem to be sure of are
certain properties of certain hypothetical
atoms and molecules as these are taken to

exist in 'matter'; and sundry stresses, transverse vibrations, or undulations of a certain hypothetical 'medium'—his remark will probably be taken as the measure of his ignorance. If he further presume, in his unscientific way, to imagine that, of the two, we could more readily dispense with matter than with energy, he will again be charged with ignorance. He may, however, console himself with the reflection that since there is, for scientist as for himself, unquestionable reality behind 'matter,' whatever matter be, so there is indubitable reality behind energy, whatever energy be. Further, that this reality is proven to him by the way in which the phenomena of matter and energy affect his consciousness, just as the reality of his limbs is proven to him. The evidence is practically the same all round. If he does not feel called upon to abandon the reality of his body and bodily movements, neither need he relinquish the reality of any external object or force, provided the evidence for it in consciousness is sufficient.

We therefore submit that, for all manifestations of energy, as for all material phenomena—that is, for the physical universe,
so far as it is cognisable by man—we are
fully entitled to postulate Reality, and that
its natural place is first in our series. In
reference to ourselves and an external world,
conception is at one end of the chain, reality
at the other, consciousness is between: on
one hand, consciousness formulates or 'pro-
jects' conceptions—on the other, it receives
and operates on external influences (excitants)
emanating from reality. And thus we are
linked with the universe.

*　*　*　*　*

7: UNIFICATION OF REALITY.

Going back now for a moment to the
corpuscular theory of matter which, until
science pronounces differently, we of course
loyally abide by, the question arises whether
we are to regard every material object, which
our senses note, as having an independent

and isolated reality.   If chair, table, orange, has each its separate reality, then so has every leaf in the forest, every blade of grass, every grain of sand by the seashore, every particle of vapour or gas, and (taking them as entities) every atom of matter and every imaginable division of ether.   On this line, we fill the universe with inconceivable hosts of separate realities.   This, again, is perhaps the nonsense of the layman.   But he does not commit it: he is continually combining and unifying his myriads.   Behind the forest, with its innumerable details, he puts a single reality; he sees but one reality behind the sand of seashore, desert, and rock; one serves him for water in all its forms, and one for a man though made up of uncountable cells.   And the step from this process of unification, to the conception of one universal reality underlying all which meets his senses, may be rapidly and surely taken.

As with matter, so with energy; only that, thanks to modern science, in framing a conception of energy we seem to arrive at the

idea of unity more quickly. Starting in
infancy, probably from such notions of force
as the exercise of a childish volition and the
use of puny muscles give us, we are soon
educated to a perception of the infinitely
greater forces which surround us, and are
ready to follow the astronomer who demonstrates an 'Universe in motion,' and the
physicist who is reducing all forms of energy
to motion. Leaders of thought who stretch
our ideas thus widely have none the less, like
ourselves, had to begin from the same humble
basis of conceptions arising in an infantile
consciousness. The astronomer, who is using
the diameter of the earth's orbit as a base-
line and calculating distance by light-years,
took his earliest conceptions of space and time
from the dimensions of his nursery and a
hungry waiting for his dinner. The physicist,
who is now solving the problems of motion,
gathered his early notions from the spin of
his top and the roll of his marbles. Leverrier
and Adams, who won the blue ribbon of their
age by the prediction of Neptune, had to learn

to count five on their baby fingers, like the rest of us. From infancy to maturity, from the smallest to the greatest which comes within our ken, we have to build up our conceptions of external objects and forces from the impressions which reach consciousness, much in the same way as the astronomer builds up, from a yard-measure, the base-line which is to help him to determine the parallax of a distant star. Measurements of distance, calculations of mass, time, and force, have constantly to be verified and checked, even for the most experienced, by fresh observations, and these, like all before, depend greatly on the validity of sense-perceptions.

Thus we come back to our contention, viz., that the proof of existence for anything external to us, whether it relates to matter or force, rests ultimately on the testimony of consciousness; and this, because man is such as he is—'ἄνθρωπος': as effectually shut up in his anthropism, as an ox in its bovism, or a dog in its canism. This need not prevent

him from using his faculties as far as ever
they will go : their range is not reached until
the latest data, by the ablest experts aided by
the most finished instruments, have been
gathered. But all such data, from the earliest
to the latest, must in the first instance pass
through the narrow gateways which lead into
the court of consciousness, and it is from the
testimony presented in that court, when compared with and checked by previous and
collateral testimony, that the value of all data
referring to an external world is determined.
For *reality* in the sources from which such
data originate we have to trust to the same
evidence we unhesitatingly accept for personal
existence : not so intimate and immediately
convincing, it may be, but clearly of the very
same nature, and of the only kind our anthropism permits. Thus for Reality underlying every manifestation of matter and energy
that reaches us, we rest our case, and with
confidence, on precisely the same description
of evidence which convinces us of the reality

of our bodily existence. They stand or fall together. The same holds good for the phenomena of psychism.

If it be objected that, with so wide a generalisation in view, it is absurd to start from so humble an object as an orange, our reply is that any complete examination of that homely fruit will, in the end, lead on to the problems of the universe as inevitably as does the telescope of the astronomer. In addition to the physics of an orange, we may also bear in mind that a single pip involves the enigma of life, and carries us back to the earliest mystery of protoplasm. Had a scientist condescended to take our route, his purpose could have been equally served by a pebble from the roadside, the petal of a flower, the dust from a bit of chalk, or the impress on a photographic film from a star too distant to be ever seen by mortal eye.

CHAPTER IV.

THEORY OF A SUPREME NOUMENON.

"Homo sum; humani nihil a me alienum puto."

If only one could 'try on' a few minds. Burns wrote

> "O wad some Power the giftie gie us
> To see oursel's as ithers see us!"

A candid neighbour sometimes helps us to a brief possession of that "giftie," and the effect is wholesome. But the other one? Fancy its surprises and lessons. A very interesting revelation would be the varying way in which different minds regard a supreme Noumenon. It is one on which men seldom tell their inmost thought—not the men whom one would like to hear; yet in dumb or articulate fashion, the human mind has always been

1

more or less occupied with it.   Primitive men
have found it in anything stronger or craftier
than themselves : philosophers have searched
all Nature, including their own, with strange
and conflicting results.   Some have contended
that, since the mere existence of such Noumenon is a point we can never make sure of,
enquiry is arrested from the beginning: others,
admitting its existence, have pronounced its
nature and operation to be utterly unknowable,
and therefore not open to investigation : many
have thought that most information is to be
gained by questioning sacred books and tra-
ditions.   It does not fall within our present
scheme to enquire from authority and tradition,
and we have neither competence nor leisure
for " chasing the Absolute through the libraries
of Europe."   We must therefore limit ourselves to a brief examination of some of the
commoner theories.   So far as it is applicable,
we propose to follow the same naturalistic
method as in the preceding chapter.

Many will refuse to advance beyond the
point therein reached.   Accepting the evidence

as we have it, they hold that the way is blocked
when we come to the universal Reality which
underlies all phenomena. They contend that
since this Reality is intangible, invisible, quite
inaccessible by the only route open to us, we
must be satisfied with its simple recognition,
and resign ourselves, with such patience as
we can muster, to the nescience of Agnosticism.
We agree as to the blocking of that particular
road, but in entering it, the avowed object
was to trace out only one mental process.
This we think has been fairly accomplished,
and until it is ascertained that no flank-path
is available, we are not inclined to abandon
the journey. Though we must regard the
sense-impression route as the sole natural
channel through which information from an
external world can reach us, we also remember
that every item which arrives by this route
has to pass under the scrutiny of reason. A
judge sits in the court of consciousness, incor-
ruptible, vigilant, ever ready to lay bare the
imperfection and fallacy which beset even the
most painstaking testimony; appealed to, be

it observed, by none more eagerly and confi-
dently than by those very scientists who collect
the bulk and best of our evidence.

It would be a serious mistake, however, to
suppose that this judge has nothing else to do
but weigh sense-evidence. His business is
extensive and various. It falls within his
province, for instance, to decide about the
validity of a document we picked up, just as
the big rock came into view. There is no
name to it, and it has evidently been dropped
by some previous traveller who, like ourselves,
has found the way obstructed. He seems to
have been engaged in a similar enquiry, and
he comments as follows :—

Here we appear to have the universal
Reality or Noumenon which underlies
and explains all the phenomena of
matter, energy, and intelligence we
have met with. We can neither get
past it nor explore it, but it seems
reasonable to believe two things about
it ;—

First; that the phenomena in question are ultimately dependent on, and

manifestations of, this supreme Reality. With this goes, of course, the corollary that man, though for himself and so far as he knows, the most important item in the universe, is yet but one amongst many phenomena, dependent and related like the rest.

Second ; that, taking the universe, in so far as our feeble powers can grapple with it, as in some sort a measure of duration, magnitude, and force, the Reality on which it depends must at least equal it. But we can assign no limits to the universe, and therefore none to the Reality on which it depends. From this position to the acceptance of eternity, universal presence, and un-bounded power in such Reality, the step is not a long one. And if, as some contend, we find in this same Reality the source of that consummate intelli-gence which is everywhere manifest, we are not far from conclusions which are satisfactory to reason and, at the same time, in harmony with science.

So much for the document. Should its deductions be approved by the judge who has

to test them, it is clear we are in possession
of certain definite and valuable knowledge
respecting the great Noumenon we are considering: a knowledge of existence, manifestation, attribute, and relation, which cannot
fail to influence the entire attitude of thought
in those who accept it. Possessed of such
knowledge, we can afford to look calmly on
that frowning and unapproachable "Unknowable" which today is paraded in our midst,
robed in the ineffable garb of an adjective to
which a restricted and half-technical significance has been given by certain 'illuminati,'
and for which older and equally expressive
terms (incomprehensible, inscrutable, un-
searchable) have been roughly pushed aside.
Comprehension there can never be for man,
apprehension there may be. Though possessed, as he thinks, of the knowledge in
question, even the simplest theist adds to it
the conviction that the Supreme and Eternal
Power which he humbly recognises, is, in its
nature, utterly inscrutable and incomprehensible. We who have not yet emerged

from " Naturalism," and plume ourselves on
exactness of thought, can certainly in this
instance lay no claim to priority or greater
definiteness. Let us at least be honest, and
confess that the limitation of our knowledge
in the direction we are considering, so strongly
emphasised by the fashionable agnosticism of
the day, was insisted on by eastern sages long
ago. Zophar the Naamathite, and Professor
Huxley are at one on the point. When the
ocean can be held in a winecup, when an ant
can expound the planet on which it creeps,
when man can pass the inexorable limit which
his anthropism imposes, then perhaps we may
find some bridge across the impassible gulf
which divides finite from infinite.

But we are anticipating. We wish to be
quite frank, and therefore admit at once that
the universal Reality underlying physical
phenomena, even if accepted, can become a
causal and ruling Noumenon only by theory.
There is no inevitable transition. A monistic
manœuvre might effect it, or the two deductions of the document we found, but in either

case we have to change rails. When Faraday
quitted his week-day hard-headed, proof-
demanding scientific labour, to conduct the
Sunday contemplations of an obscure and
peculiar religious sect, he must surely have
opened an altogether distinct chamber in his
mind, reserved strictly for such occasions.
The agnostic chemist who is examining a
lump of sulphur or chalk may accept a reality
behind the group of phenomena he is investi-
gating, and may even agree to its being considered a part of one universal Reality; but
when his philosophic friend proceeds to adorn
this with the regal robe of final and intelligent
causation, he may well cry, " Halt there. You
are wandering into an entirely different region,
and the road does not go through my laboratory. If you find anything interesting I shall
be glad to hear of it; in the meantime, I
stick to my reagents and lenses." Nor can
we be surprised that the literary agnostic also
should have grown distrustful of philosophy
and logic. He may have learned their weakness by experience. None the less, we think

that agnosticism, as in popular vogue, has gone far past its legitimate scientific use, and has itself set up as a full-blown philosophy of doubt and negation. We place it with other views for examination.

With regard to the conversion of Reality (Noumenon) behind phenomena, as accepted by an agnostic scientist, into the ennobled form which it must assume, as we think, before it becomes adequate, one further remark should, however, be made. Psychic phenomena have to be accounted for as well as physical phenomena: they cannot be investigated in a laboratory, and they equally imply a noumenon. If the Reality or Noumenon which underlies the phenomena of matter, energy, and psychism be unknown and unknowable, it is just as unwarrantable to assume that it is physical as that it is psychic. It may be both, or neither, but it must include both; unless a myth, it must be held capable of producing both. We recall the fact that the most exalted phenomenon we know, viz., man, exemplifies in

a very striking way the close association
(dualism) or unity (monism) of mind and
matter. It is precisely his psychism which
gives man his superiority, and in his double
nature we see, as we think, a strong analogical
warrant for the inclusion of what is psychic,
as well as what is physical, in a basal Reality
or Noumenon. As will be shown presently,
the anthropomorphism involved in such conception need not trouble us in the least.
Nor is there much danger of being caught in
the obsolete 'mind-stuff' trap: in these
protoplasmic days, we fancy it is nearly
abandoned. 'Mind-stuff' is now a phenomenon only, and, for the biologist, means
brain-stuff, of man and animal. Noumenon
was there and busy long before the appearance
of the particular phenomenon, protoplasm,
whether neural or ante-neural: so also, in our
opinion, were psychic phenomena. As already
stated, we consider the view untenable which
limits these to what the protoplasmic mind
has to show.

Figure 5.

(Conception of Supreme or Universal Noumenon).

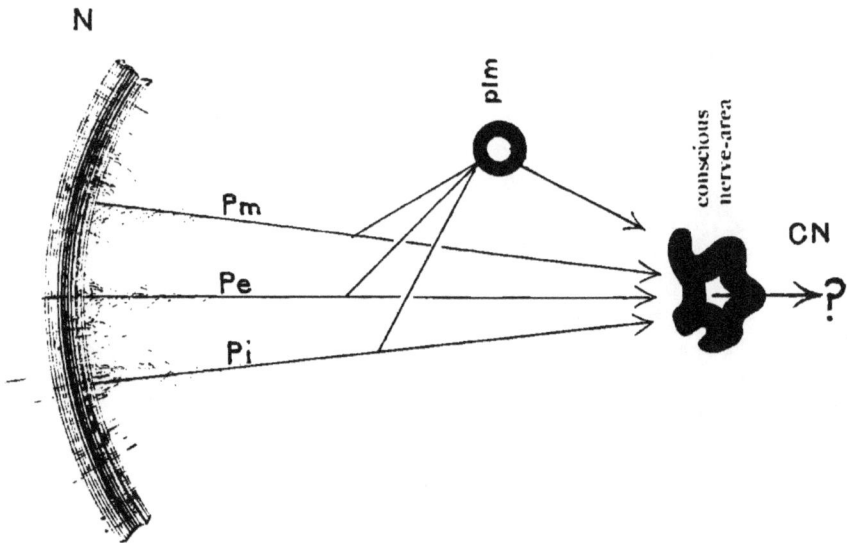

N.   Supreme Noumenon.

Pm.   Phenomena of matter.

Pe.   ,,   ,, energy.

Pi.   ,,   ,. intelligence, general and
                        protoplasmic.

plm.   Protoplasmic mind.

CN.   Conception of Supreme Noumenon.

On these grounds we submit that, though the agnostic scientist, ruled by his sense-habit, may content himself with a physical Noumenon, the agnostic philosopher, having psychism on his hands, must adopt a Noumenon which includes this. It is this complete form we have now to examine, and we venture on a somewhat risky diagram which may serve as text. See Figure 5, opposite.

*   *   *   *   *

N is represented by a broad radiating curve, taken as part of a circle or sphere embracing the universe. This, of course, is sheer phantasy, and hopelessly vitiated by the limitation which occurs whenever a circle is drawn, with whatever radius. Circles, however, are favourite symbols, often used in science; for instance, by physicists and chemists, when trying to make us understand the ways and wars and compacts of hypo-thetical atoms. To ordinary eyes, the sun is a circle or disc which may be covered by a penny: since its recent eclipse, however, astronomers have once more been telling us of its vast dimensions, as they told us long ago of its ancient nebular area, planet-progeny, and sway throughout the sun-realm. By supposition, let our circle be as a sun to the universe, and draw it with an infinite radius.

Pm, Pe, Pi, represent the phenomena of the universe as we are cognisant of them. How we construe them in detail is shown in Figure 3 (page 58). Amongst them is the protoplasmic mind of animal and man (**plm**), every human mind, except his own, being objective to each subjective observer: indeed, the introspective faculty of consciousness gives it the power of observing even itself. All phenomena are held to emanate from the Supreme Noumenon, however long and devious the route by which they reach the observer. They may possibly concern other beings beside the conceited inhabitants of our little planet, and be differently presented.

It is clear that any, or all phenomena, if regarded as manifestations of an eternal Noumenon, may themselves be eternal, yet dependent. It also becomes indifferent whether we view life and psychism (animal or human) as direct emanations from such Noumenon, or as the result of synthesis, *modo evolutionis*, amongst phenomena. Further, when phenomena are once relegated to their normal and subordinate position, we can afford to be very liberal to the Materialist in the matter of 'potentialities,' and can welcome the most startling discoveries of evolution. They are only adding to our small knowledge of the ways of the Supreme Evolver: we are under no compulsion to declare paper and printing of the book we are reading to be, not only book itself, but also author.

CN stands for conception of the Universal Noumenon, and is represented by the symbol of interrogation (?). As well it may. Here is a conception we can neither formulate nor 'project,' and the attempt of our Figure is confessedly a failure. Yet the mind of man has been trying to frame such a conception in every place and age of which we have a

record. Small blame to the ignorant savage
with his wooden god. Feebly lit, he
is unconsciously struggling with the same
problem as the old Hebrew prophet and the
encyclopædic professor at Oxford. Small
blame to any of them for the anthropomorphism which beguiles them, unless to be
human is a reproach. The most attenuated
abstraction of the metaphysician is as strictly
anthropic as is the crudest conception of the
latest recruit in the ' salvation army.'

We put the theistic conception with the
rest. It is far too important and widely held
to be lightly dealt with, but as we do not
here enquire what a special revelation teaches,
we can discuss the conception only from a
naturalistic point of view. We are justified
in doing this, for even such revelation has
admittedly, with one solitary exception, come
through man *to* man, and is therefore deeply
tinged with the anthropism of both medium
and receiver. And as to the exception, what
can be more anthropomorphic than the
opening words of the prayer enjoined, as a

pattern, by the greatest Teacher the world has ever had. So also, nearly 2000 years later, for such as can read between the lines, is the summing-up of a renowned philosopher (Mr. Spencer, quoted at p. 170).

We have seen (Chap. II.) how far modern science, aided by its interpreter, evolution, can help us in framing a conception of a supreme Noumenon. In these latter days, choice seems to be narrowing. To return to our diagram, **CN** may represent **N** as,—

1. **Non-existent (Atheism). The fool - negation. Rare.**
2. **Unknowable (Agnosticism). Noun or adjective: taken as adjective and with ' incomprehensible ' for synonym, we are all agnostic.**
3. **Energised Matter (Materialism). Primal matter with ' potentialities ': protyle and power. Is expressed by the equation ... Matter + physical energy + evolution = universe. Evolution either a potentiality of matter or a special form of physical energy, and capable of producing psychism.**

4. **Syndicate of matter, energy, and intelligence (Pantheism).**

5. **" Infinite and Eternal Energy, from which all things proceed " (Spencerism).**

6. **ΘΕΌΣ (Theism).**

Each thinker will choose for himself. They are all anthropic and all, except the first, more or less anthropomorphic. Whoever adopts the last (theistic) conception may, however, laugh at the bogey of anthropomorphism, or its variant " idiomorphism." Why hesitate? Put in a ' t ' at once, and let it then be, for the wonderful people whom it imposes on, an appropriate estimate of the view held by, say, an Archbishop of Canterbury, or call it the stupefying drug which befogs the understanding of the multitude. Looked at closely, the scarecrow of anthropomorphism is really a poor affair. A celebrated writer of the first century says, in one place, " I speak as a man "; in another, " I speak as a fool." On the present issue, or on any, we can think and speak only in one or other of these capacities. Man's perceptions, ideas, language, necessarily remain anthropic, whether for an orange or a Deity. He cannot pass the limits which Nature has assigned, and all his conceptions bear the inevitable mark of the instrument which produces them. His notions of existence, power, intelligence, and personality spring originally from what he observes in himself; from this he infers to what and who are external to himself. By his own sense of existence he understands existence outside himself: the personality he attributes to others is the transference of an idea springing from his own sense of personality: for appreciating an external intelligence, the only faculty he has is his own intelligence, and this, whether he knows it or not, remains virtually the measure he applies elsewhere.

Anthropomorphism infests even science. Energy, in all its forms, is tainted by it—is continually, as we say, compelling and controlling the inoffensive particles of inert matter. All conceptions of a supreme Noumenon

suffer in like manner, but we grow indignant
only when the culprit is a theist. Well,
perhaps he is the blindest sinner ; so we will
have him in the dark room and examine his
eyes. As we have no beam in our own, we
shall see clearly the mote in his.

*　　*　　*　　*　　*

A prominent, and to many, most objectionable feature in the theistic conception is,
the transference of the idea of **personality**
from man to Deity. The supreme Noumenon,
from being immaculate ' It,' has become a
debased ' He '—a sort of grand Personage
who originates, devises, and rules, like a big
man, only more so. There is a fallacy here.
We submit that ' it ' is a fraud and sneak,
doing precisely the same things which ' he ' is
condemned for. With regard to the transference in question, far from disputing it we
contend that it is harmless, natural, and due
to the inveterate habit of our mental instrument. However we account for it, there can
be little doubt that the sense of personality

is one of the strongest elements in our consciousness, if not *the* strongest : small wonder that we constantly transfer the idea it contains to the world of beings, and even of things, around us, or that language is so deeply tinctured by it. Not merely do we regard our fellow-mortals as persons like ourselves, but we personify their races, governments, institutions, dignities, and pursuits. We take a man to pieces, and personify his strength, beauty, reason, will, imagination, passion, virtue, and vice. We personify nature, science, art, even our petty inventions. For us, sun *rises*, darkness *falls*, wind *moans*, *howls*, *whispers*, sea *roars* and *rages*, light *pierces*, cold *searches*, blow *hurts*, locomotive *shrieks*, arrow *flies*, mousetrap *catches*, gold *tempts*, time *presses*, space *permits*, passion *blinds*, ambition *spurs*, thought *strikes*, *tickles*, *stings*, *oppresses*, *dazzles* : death is a reaper and carries a sickle, time is furnished with a fore-lock and wings. From being a mere convenient peg on which to hang things, Nature becomes

the most imperious and alluring of dames;
Science is a band of sisters, Art a group of
Muses. Personification filled the Olympus
of Greece and the Pantheon of Rome: a
little later, with characteristic audacity, it
converted ' Theos' Himself into ' Trinitas.'
When we come to think of it, personification
is a most useful fellow. Supplies parts to
the geometric point, rids motion of its tire-
some travelling companion, and thought of
protoplasm; sets ether trembling and em-
bodies atoms; incorporates factors, qualities,
abstractions, hypotheses; serves even the
nefarious ' It' at every turn and corner;
enables the Materialist (himself a personification) to conjure with ' protyle'; and, after
personifying Evolution for us, transforms him
into an interpreter. What harm comes of all
this? We are not deceived by the mental
trick, if it be one, any more than the scientist
is deceived by his sense-perceptions. We
are merely thinking of the things around us
in our personal way, and talking of them in
such language as we have. Doing so does

not confuse nor lessen the distinction between
ourselves and what surrounds us ; certainly
does not commit us to any admission of
likeness : the habit is simply a convenience,
or rather an exigence. If we choose to
discuss the universe and its cause, our
thoughts and language must be anthropic,
and both the one and the other are incu-
rably saturated with metaphor, imagery, and
personification, because man is such as he
is—an imaginative being and a *person.*

The chief objection to the personal constituent in a conception of Deity lies of
course in the idea of limitation, and likeness
to ourselves, which it is supposed to carry.
But does it ? When we transfer, from our
acquired mental possessions, the ideas of
power and intelligence to a conception of
Deity, limitation is at once dropped, and a
sense of contrast, rather than of likeness, is
felt. Weakness is contrasted with absolute
power, ignorance with perfect knowledge.
Much the same may be said of the idea of
personality as applied to Deity, at least

by an educated theist. Such an idea has
assuredly nothing to do with limitation.
One would scarcely be surprised if man, as
phenomenon-in-chief, did bear some impress;
but if likeness there be, so also is there
contrast and unlikeness. As we take it, the
theist is trying, in his anthropic way, to
express his conviction that Deity means
living, independent, intelligent Being; not
diffused 'Welt-geist,' nor yet non-animate,
non-intelligent force. And he draws this
contrast—ΘΕΌΣ is a Being, but eternal
and self-existent; man is also a being, but
derived, transitory, and utterly dependent:
ΘΕΌΣ is living, but the Source of life; man
is also living, but only as a drop from this
source, lodged for a moment in a morsel of
protoplasm. Thus, as with the notions of
power and intelligence, so with that of personality; likeness and limitation are lost in the
idea of infiniteness. Though not a disciple
of " Naturalism," the theist may perchance be
a naturalist, and then, in spite of his weakness
for the protoplasmic basis of life and the

limiting periphery of an organism, he will
be aware that biology is not omniscient, and
probably he will think that, even respecting
it, there is room for Hamlet's opinion of
Horatio's philosophy.

The conception of personality as applied
to Deity is valued, by those who know no
better, for another reason. It expresses a
belief in what may be called, for lack of a
fitter term, *an approachable side* in such
Deity. Very anthropomorphic no doubt,
but why unreasonable? Some sort of connexion, some line of relationship, cannot be
denied between the phenomenon, man, and
the cause of this phenomenon, be this cause
what it may—an energised 'Materies,' or
the Spencerian 'Unknowable' source of all
phenomena, or the 'Θεός' of the theist. To
some minds, such a relationship may mean
nothing more than the link between a phenomenon and its cause; it may be the
frostiest recognition of reason, the barest
instance of causation. To other minds it
may mean far more than this. Man is

an emotional and imaginative, as well as a
reasoning creature, and we cannot limit the
affair to his reason. Fear or admiration will
spring up, if the source of all phenomena be
regarded as supreme in power and wisdom;
or a sense of constant supervision and dependence, if control be looked on as incessant
and universal; and of trust, if the ruling
power be considered just and benevolent.
Moreover, since man is notoriously also a
religious animal, such nonsense as prayer,
confession, thanksgiving, &c., may seem
natural to the devout imbecile who cannot
understand that an intelligent Power is not,
as a rule, interested in its own operations,
nor that an Almighty has certainly, by his
own act and deed, made himself the slave
of unalterable laws—indeed is, as superior
people have long known, nothing more than
a ' personification ' of these laws.

Underlying all these conceptions, from the
professor's to the washerwoman's, is the
fundamental idea that man is in relation
with a supreme power or being. On man's

side, the relation is of necessity personal.
How far it shall remain so, and involve
personality in the supreme being or power,
depends on the stage of thought and the
idiosyncracy of the thinker: certainly the
relationship is personal throughout the whole
tract of thought which lies between the fetish
of the Hottentot and the purest conception
of the monotheist. Personality may be
lost in the abstraction of the metaphysician,
or the 'unknowable' of the agnostic; but
relationship is not, and it cannot be got rid
off except by denying the noumenal basis of
phenomena. We may also bear in mind
that 'Demos' has to be catered for, as well
as those who can live on Hamilton, Spencer,
Browning, or Karl Pearson. A contented
resting in abstractions is for the select few;
the popular mind refuses to be nourished on
abstractions.

* * * * *

We have spent more time on the theist
than some will think he is worth; in any
case we must now attend to his rivals.

Spencer we regard, and with all respect, as
an ally rather than a foe of theism; we have
therefore to look elsewhere, and we propose
to search the haunts of " Naturalism."   For
dialectic purposes, it is convenient and legitimate to place under the ban of " Naturalism "
sundry perverse modes of thought, and then
castigate the offenders who indulge in them.
We do not presume to criticise the distin-
guished writer who has laid the ban ; indeed,
in the first chapter, we have followed his
example.   But in belabouring Materialism,
our object has been to show, not so much
that it is wrong, as that it is inadequate.
As we are all necessarily to a considerable
extent agnostic, so are we all, in a sense,
materialist.   Even Hume jumped from the
roadway to the safe footpath, in famous
Princes Street, when a material carriage was
coming.   Why mince matters ?   Theism
itself is partly materialistic.   The crown of
theism is usually held to be Christianity, and
of this, the central truth is the ' Incarnation.'
Where—we ask with all reverence—is a

choicer example of materialism to be found ?
Deity embodied in protoplasm—"manifest in
the flesh." No doubt, as a biologic theist
might remind us, Deity is 'manifest' in an
epithelium-cell and in every man it helps to
cover, but this is a quibble which orthodoxy
would disdain. For it, "manifest in the
flesh" has a crasser meaning; more akin to
the 'hoc meum corpus est' which Luther
declined to relinquish. Can it be that such
opposed forms of thought as theism, agnosticism, and materialism (and pantheism?—
" of him, and through him, and to him ")
actually hold out a hand to each other?
Strange if true, but reassuring.

The cave of " Naturalism " is reputed to
harbour a numerous and motley population.
Two of its leading sections (materialist and
agnostic) we have sufficiently examined. The
largest tribe are the Gallios. Some years ago
Mr. Laurence Oliphant, in his " Piccadilly,"
called them " Wholly-worldlies "; at present
they are " Secularists." They are by no
means confined to the cave, indeed, there are

as many outside as in : the majority of them
are short-sighted, some very ; as a whole,
the clan is remarkable for numbers, rather
than wisdom. But they have a nucleus (or
is it a nucleolus?) of earnest, thoughtful,
philanthropic men, who redeem the character
of their tribe, and are ready, oddly enough,
to enter into alliance with ' ists ' of any sort,
theists included, who will adopt the catholic
shibboleth of providing " things honest in the
sight of all men "—things material and
ethical, for themselves and others. This
nucleus rarely quits head-quarters, and, for
the most part, holds a strong opinion on the
' Noumenon ' question; but the bulk of the
Gallios are much too engrossed with business
or fun to care about a ' Noumenon ' of any
kind ; they will adopt any or go without, just
as it happens.

It is said there are many scientists in the
cave. We believe this is a fact, but we have
nothing to do with them as scientists. Science
has no creed. She is charming but a flirt,
and will forgather with any ' ist ' whose wits

please her. "Naturalism" has certainly no
monopoly of the scientists. Many eminent
among them, past and present, have been or
are theists and even christians, and have found
no difficulty in harmonising their faith with
their science. The difficulty is therefore not
insuperable. An old-fashioned poem has the
line

"An undevout astronomer is mad."

Had the Rector of Welwyn been better informed, or more candid, he would scarcely
have penned that line, for many a very sane
and skilful star-gazer has been materialist or
agnostic. But not because he was astronomer.
A long roll, with Newton at its head, might
be cited to show that, so far as astronomy
goes, if agnosticism or materialism can be
built on science, so equally can theism. The
same holds good for all branches of science.[1]

---

[1] The late Mr. Romanes, himself at one time
agnostic and almost materialist, writes as follows in his
"Thoughts on Religion" (page 137), published (1895)
after his death :—

"Thus, if we look to the greatest mathematicians in

There are some minor groups—positivists, determinists, pantheists, &c.—but their numbers are small, and they are not influential. Asia is the proper home of pantheism : there it has millions of followers, but in the locality we are examining it is represented only by a few cranks, known as 'esoteric Buddhists.'

We must not forget the oldest inhabitant. His race may at one time have been sturdy, but the 'struggle for existence' has been too much for him ; he is a mere survival. We refer to the Atheist : not, of course, to the man so-labelled, but to him who holds his

---

the world's history, we find Kepler and Newton as Christians ; La Place, on the other hand, an infidel. Or, coming to our own times, and confining our attention to the principal seat of mathematical study :—when I was at Cambridge, there was a galaxy of genius in that department emanating from that place such as had never before been equalled. And the curious thing in our present connexion is that all the most illustrious names were ranged on the side of orthodoxy. Sir W. Thomson, Sir George Stokes, Professors Tait, Adams, Clerk-Maxwell, and Cayley—not to mention a number of lesser lights, such as Routh, Todhunter, Ferrers, &c.— were all avowed Christians."

view after due thought; to such we concede
honesty, but diagnose mental climacterism.
Doubters abound in the cave, but not deniers :
non-theists are in plenty, but non-theism is
not atheism; a difference, as well as a distinction, if you please.   Christians were called
atheists by supercilious Romans who would
not take the trouble to understand them.   It
is not surprising that men like Tyndall and
Huxley resented the nickname; they had too
much brain to be atheists.

For our own part, we would rather build
up than destroy.   The proper antithesis to
' Naturalism,' we submit, is not theism but
Supernaturalism, and as such, not the an-
tagonist, but the complement of ' naturalism.'
We are inclined to think that, nowadays,
there are but few who seriously regard Nature
as a self-constituted, self-regulative Automatism, working forever in a closed cycle of
evolution and devolution.   For most there
is some sort of supreme originating and
administrative Power, which Nature, as or-
dinarily understood, does not supply.   Such

Power is variously named and appraised, but it is essentially Super-nature. Where it is not accepted, all sorts of ' potentialities ' have to be smuggled in under the elastic cover of evolution; and physical energy, hiding in the convenient shelter of an ' unknowable ' mist, has to be stretched until it is expanded into the all-sufficing, all-fulfilling Power of Spencer. If a venture of our own can be tolerated, we would suggest that, by combining the "Supreme Mind " of Plato with the " Infinite and Eternal Energy " of Spencer, we reach a conception which is adequate, and which need not offend either theist or non-theist.

*   *   *   *   *

After all, conduct is greater than creed; the latter is important chiefly as it influences conduct. Stuart Mill says, " One man with a belief is worth two with opinions." In a sense this is true enough, especially for fighting purposes, but opinion and belief are merely different stages of the same thing, and neither is of much value unless founded on

reason. Faith not resting on reason is credu-
lity ; is just as objectionable as the incredulity
which will not yield to reason. Unfortunately,
one's respect for creeds and beliefs is diminished when one comes to think how, for the
most part, they are determined. What a
man believes depends far more on the country
and race to which he belongs, on the times
in which he lives, on parentage, training,
temperament, and individual experience of
life, than on any process of reasoning. He is
a christian, mohammedan, buddhist, or wor-
shipper of sticks and stones, chiefly because
he belongs to this or that country and people.
In Europe and America Christianity is the
dominant creed, but here again its adoption
is largely a matter of birthplace and race.
Though christian enough to be classified as
such in Whitaker's almanack, a large majority
of the inhabitants of both continents admittedly hold their creed in very languid fashion ;
they have it because it is prevalent, just as
they put on the same clothes, live in the same
houses, and adopt the same pursuits and

L

habits as their neighbours. By none is this
indifference more clearly seen, and keenly
felt, than by that earnest and convinced
minority without which the creed would
perish.

The very incomplete success of christianity,
after nineteen centuries, is usually attributed
to the wickedness of man's heart : we venture
to suggest it is due partly also to the fact that
his reason has not been more fully won.
Whether this be owing to defect in teaching
or dulness in learning we leave others to
decide, but it is clear that, hitherto, men have
learnt very partially and very slowly. The
result is that the christian faith, instead of
being for all its adherents the living force it
should be, is professed by many on account
of its current respectability, and by not a few
as a mere compromise, an 'in case' for
possible eventualities. Is proof demanded?
Then enquire in London or Paris or Berlin
or St. Petersburg or New York or Chicago.
Their senates, municipalities, bourses, com-
merce, amusements, literature, streets, palaces,

prisons, slums, yield proof enough; and
country tells the same tale as chief city, if less
noisily. At the present moment (March,
1898) we have the five or six leading christian
powers of the world jealously watching each
other, preparing for a wild and bloody scramble
for what does not belong to any of them.
Verily a fine object-lesson for the disciples of
Confucius and the worshippers of Mumbo
Jumbo! At best, internecine amenities are
held to be sufficiently safeguarded by the
" do ut des " principle of " Broker " Bismarck.
But christianity is not intended to meet inter-
national difficulties? Good. Note its influence, then, on men in smaller groups or
individually. It is a commonplace that com-
mittees, companies, boards, syndicates, are
infested by the demons of log-rolling and
' exploitage.' " Every man for himself and
devil take the hindmost" is an ordinary
maxim of mercantile life. ' Caveat emptor '
serves the London tradesman just as it helped
the Roman shopkeeper 2000 years ago. " Do
unto others as . . . . . . they do unto you" is

held by many to be good enough, even for
friends. The gracious insertion—" as ye
would they should do "—which christianity
makes, is a counsel of perfection fit only for
dreamers. Forgive your enemies ? Nay, we
find the prickly motto of Scotland more useful.
Turn the other cheek to the smiter ? Well,
yes—just to see if he means it; but if he hits
that too, then go for him. Take the two
precepts which sum up the code of theo-
christianity. "Thou shalt love the Lord thy
God with all thy heart," &c., "and thy
neighbour as thyself." What proportion of
Whitaker's 448 millions of Christians, of
London's six millions, even pretend to observe
these precepts ? Dread God—think as little
about Him as possible—sometimes get so far
as to trust Him—but _love_ Him, and in the
formidable measure required ? And the neigh-
bour-law—who obeys it ? One per cent, one
tenth per cent, of nominal christians ? The
average christian, like the average man, loves
and cherishes himself profoundly and constantly, as indeed he must if he would

'survive': in happy families, christian and not, there is much love for husband, wife, children, and parents. But the neighbour— how much for him? The moiety demanded? Surely the Devil laughs at the paltry quotient forthcoming. Think for a moment of the omissions and commissions of our own most christian community. Of the foul courts and alleys in our large towns; of the grinding miseries of the poor; of the dens of vice and corruption; of the army of loafers and criminals; of the mad and fevered race for wealth; of the deceptions and trickeries which disgrace our trades and professions; of the selfish frivolity which marks so many of our pleasures and pursuits; of the meannesses, hypocrisies, low motives and aims which disfigure the daily walk and life of Britain's forty millions of Whitaker-christians. If the superficies of statistical christianity be scarcely satisfactory for the end of the 19th century, we certainly do not derive much comfort by plumbing its depth, even in a part where our insular vanity thinks it deepest. Far be it from us to speak slightingly of real christians and their work. They are the very salt of the earth, and their loving unceasing labour for others is the despair and admiration of lazy critics, but the disproportion between harvest and labourers is too marked, the apathy of nominals too glaring, to escape notice.

This is the seamy side on which pessimism delights to dwell; happily there is another whereon moral beauty and noble effort are just as distinctly inscribed, nor can there be any doubt how greatly these are fostered by christianity. Though it is sometimes credited with ameliorations which are due rather to the advance of science and civilisation, we hold it to be the most powerful factor for good which has yet appeared among men, and only regret that its advance should be hindered through lack of a closer alliance between faith and reason. Compare for instance what is, with what might be, the influence of just one elementary tenet, viz., the belief in a future life wherein happiness or misery will depend on conduct in the present life. Man is,

amongst other things, a forecasting and prudent creature ; he strives to ensure himself
against future contingencies, and the greater
their probability and importance, the greater
is his self-protective effort : as Bishop Butler
said, probability is the very guide of his life.
Can we doubt what would be the result, in
average men and women, if they were at all
certain that a future life and a strict reckoning
awaited them ?   It is because they do not
believe that they do not care.   For ourselves
we have found sufficient proof, though not
easily.   In searching for it and other things,
we have grown persuaded that unconvinced
reason, quite as much as evil disposition, is at
the bottom of the impatience with which the
message from the chancel is listened to.
Surely our experience in mundane matters—
the Bishop quotes it—bears this out.   When
once the understanding is informed and convinced, the lessons of life are usually accepted
without demur.   A man will hearken to his
lawyer or his doctor, and if his judgment be
satisfied, will follow their advice, often with

pathetic docility. Why will he not listen to
his priest? Of course many do, but the
majority do not; why? As we think, because
he does not succeed in proving his case.
Excellent things in their way are imposing
fane and ritual, captivating music, impassioned
appeal to feeling and imagination; still more
excellent is the contagion of good example
and consistent life; but reason will not abdi-
cate at the bidding of any of these counsellors.

We have no desire to exalt this royal
faculty unduly. The repulsive bawd set up
by an infuriated French mob was certain
to be presently cast back into the gutter;
there is perhaps scarcely more chance of
general and ultimate acceptance for the
scornful rationalism which preceded and
followed that infamous travesty: but doubt
and indifference abound, and will probably
continue to do so until the intelligence of man
is more fully enlisted against them. The
view is heterodox, yet it seems just as
necessary to carry the intellect of man as to
win his emotional side, if the success of theo-

christianity is to be complete and lasting.
Of all the great Faiths which have swayed
mankind in the past, or still prevail, it is the
only one which has come in close contact
with science, and she will certainly not omit
her search-light in deference to authority and
tradition : for these, her respect is quite
limited. 'No one wishes her to omit,' say
some ; 'we have no fear for the truth, but let
science stick to her domain, and leave us to
our's.' That is just what she will not do :
the inquisitive jade insists on peering into
everything which interests her ; she will not
stop to ask whom it belongs to, and indeed
religion has set her the bad example of universal interference. They have quarrelled in
the past and are quarrelling still, but there
is no necessity for unending border-warfare.
Both domains are required to meet the wants
of man's complex nature, and many hope for
an eventual peaceful union. In the meantime, as we think, the christian priest is
contending at a disadvantage for want of a
few modern scientific weapons. Will not the

christian master of science give a little more
assistance ?   He is about, and notable enough,
but he is modest, and his tendency is to
abstain from any field in which he does not
consider himself an expert.   In the present
instance he could help greatly, for he alone
has exact knowledge of the enemy's strength :
he is man as well as scientist, and humanity,
even in its religious perplexities, has a claim
upon him.   Will he tell us clearly and frankly
why and how far he believes, and so help on
a considerable body of honest, ill-informed
gropers ?

*   *   *   *   *

But we are off the track : there are so
many inviting side-paths.   We shall regain it
most quickly by returning for a moment to
the cave.   There is a report that this contains
treasures as well as men.   Intellect is undoubtedly found there ; so also is worth of
character.   Its inmates further allege the
possession of ethics, morality, conscience, a
sense of duty and responsibility, and a few go

so far as to claim even natural religion.
Their opponents say they have stolen these
good things, but this they strenuously deny,
and sometimes hurl back an indignant ' tu
quoque.' If they really have these treasures,
we care not a fig how they came by them.
By evolution? By revelation?—What does
it matter? All is revelation, all is evolution,
determined by Super-nature.

The present moral condition of man
is held, by the evolutionist, to mark the
level to which he has as yet risen from a
lower and brutish stage. The theologian
regards it as the degradation of an originally
pure and innocent being, for whose restoration
a remedial process is slowly operating. Which-
ever view be taken, a strong religious instinct
in man, past and present, can scarcely be
denied. How it arose is really of little consequence. Out of dreams, shadows, ghosts,
nature's thunders, respect for ancestors and
heroes ; from intuition, from revelation ?
Again, what does it matter? The evolutionist is prepared to expect the grandest

outcome from the feeblest beginning. Man
has maybe come from an ape; we know for
certain that he starts everyday from a cell.
His religion may have commenced in the
fancies of a dream, in the watching of a
shadow, in dismay at the tempest, but neither
he nor his religion need be ashamed of an
humble origin; its humbleness is, after all,
only a human notion. The simplest cell, the
faintest gleam of moral light, equally demand
a superhuman origin, and nothing is either
small or great to an infinite Evolver. Man
does not remain a cell, nor his religion a
dream. Both grow, even as evolution has
had to do. ' Omne vivum ex ovo ' was not
reached in a day, and there is a long step
between it and Spencer's all-embracing
theories.

It is worth while to look a little more
closely at the treasures of the cave-men. The
evolutionist does not go far in his study of
man before he stumbles on *a conscience*. He
may even fancy to catch glimpses of such a
faculty before he gets to the human animal,

but in man it is soon pronounced and operative. Whence comes it? From the improving stress of environment; from the exigencies of family, tribal, communal relations; as a special ray from a supreme 'Noumenon'? It matters not: better follow Newton's example and study what and how, rather than whence; though indeed, on our theory, whence is plain enough. However accounted for, conscience remains as much a fact in evolution as is the man who possesses it. Here comes a queer, but welcome note of agreement between naturalist and supernaturalist. The existence of conscience, with whatever origin, is admitted—nay, eagerly claimed—by materialist, agnostic, secularist, and theist alike. They may call it by different names, and differ as to sanctions, but they all recognise the faculty, and insist on its importance. We have no space here for a dissection of conscience, and it needs no panegyric. It is sufficient to find in it the basis on which self-discipline rests, and the source of that sense of duty and responsibility to self,

kindred, and community, which is, at once,
the best present help we have for humanity
and the best augury for its future.   Let the
utilitarian call it 'enlightened self-interest' if
he pleases.   He has warrant both in nature
and revelation.   In the " Beatitudes," this
and that condition or act is declared " blessed "
—why? : not because it is good in itself or
does good to others, but because ' great is the
reward ' attached to it.   In like manner,
evolution insists on discipline and endurance,
if ' number one ' is to be rewarded.   But
both nature and super-nature provide for the
gregariousness of man.   Let him do good to
himself—in physical and moral health ; in
wealth, mental, ethical, or metallic—and he
cannot help at the same time doing good to
others.   In return, the communal conscience
benefits each individual.   Self-interest and
other-interest thus complete and correct each
other.   Turned inwards, conscience benefits
its possessor ; turned outwards, it prompts to
altruism.

*   *   *   *   *

There is another weighty matter on which, as we think, nature and super-nature agree : it arises out of the ' environment ' in which man is found. Everywhere he is surrounded by laws to which he has to accommodate himself. It makes no difference whether these be taken in a forensic or scientific sense : there they are, and man must obey or suffer. Laws of physics, chemistry, and biology ; laws affecting body, mind, and estate ; laws of health and morality, of civic and social life : he is encompassed by them, and woe betide him if he be ignorant or negligent. These laws are conditions of environment, and come into play in the course of evolution. The supernaturalist would probably add, they are therefore manifestations of the supreme will which expresses itself in evolution ; but waiving this, we point out that many of the cave-dwellers unreservedly admit these laws, and insist on the imperative necessity for knowing and observing them. It would be easy to draw up a decalogue to which most would subscribe—

Beware of false gods. Worship
neither wealth, nor power, nor fame,
nor science, nor business, nor pleasure,
nor man, nor nature. Bow only to the
Supreme Power on which thou art
dependent. Thou shalt inform thyself
on the laws which surround and
control thee, and obey them, for
ignorance and disobedience will not
pass unvisited. Thou shalt be clean,
active, temperate in all things, or thy
health will suffer. Thou shalt be
diligent in business, true and honour-
able in thy dealings, for in industry
and probity is welfare for thee and
others. Incessant toil is, nevertheless,
bad for thee, therefore thou shalt rest
one day in seven ; what is good for
thee is good also for thy servants ; see
to it thou art not a humbug, resting
thyself but compelling thy slaves to
go on working. Thou shalt honour
thy parents, lest thy children dishonour
thee. Thou shalt not steal, nor murder,
nor commit adultery, nor covet thy

neighbour's possessions, nor tell lies about him. Thou shalt be merciful to the poor and unfortunate, for one day thou also may need help and mercy.

Such a code includes a large slice of the "whole duty of man," yet it is common property, enjoined by all respectable 'ists.' Whilst some are rejoicing, with Arnold, over this "stream of tendency which makes for righteousness," the benighted theist rubs his eyes and exclaims, "Bless me! why all these things are written down in my book, and here are these fellows finding them out without once opening the book." The simple soul has got such a trick of looking straight to the top that he never sees the ladder. Very wrong of him. Much better be well acquainted with every rung of the ladder, than know or care where it goes to: besides, it can be far better studied lying on the ground than reared up. His first mistake betrays him into a second. His habit of ignoring the road up leads him to take his laws straight from the top, and then his head

M

gets dizzy. What if the laws concern, not
only himself and his neighbours, but also
the lawgiver, who, having issued them, can
scarcely be indifferent as to their observance.
" What a fool you are," says the evolutionist,
" nobody knows anything about a lawgiver,
and never will. Why cannot you be content,
like other folks, to pick up your conscience
where you find it, and apply it where it is
wanted. The laws are lying all round you ;
learn them and obey them, or go to the
devil."—"Just what my book says, only its
language is milder." Odd that he should
come to sound conclusions by so ludicrous
a method.

*   *   *   *   *

It will probably be agreed that, amongst
the followers of " Naturalism," there are
many who are not only earnest thinkers but
exemplary moralists, and not a few who
pride themselves on the imperative and
urgent view they take of duty and responsibility. For all such there is common ground

on which, we suggest, the theist may also be allowed standing-room. Let us, in conclusion, try to measure it :—

1. **There exists a supreme power.**
2. **The universe (including man) is the manifestation of this power—therefore dependent on it.**
3. **Man is surrounded by laws, physical and moral, and his interest lies in knowing and obeying them.**
4. **In man there is a regulative faculty called conscience, operating on himself and influencing his conduct to others.**

These four propositions are pretty generally held by non-theists, as well as theists : we submit that they form an excellent basis for natural religion. We are going to add a fifth, deduced from the preceding. It is tinged with anthropomorphism, but as to that, for reasons already given, we are entirely careless. We think that at least some non-theists can accept it, and we leave it to the judgment of the reader, if there happen to be one.   It is this—

5. **The laws which concern man, and the conscience found in him, being as strictly manifestations of the supreme power as anything else in the universe; furthermore, they being of the nature of conditions to be fulfilled or directors to be followed, man is not in his legitimate position until he accepts these conditions and obeys these mandates. When he does this completely, he is in harmony with, and obedient to the 'Voluntas' expressed in them; he is perfect, so far as his enlightenment and development permit; if a non-theist, he is at least a good man; if a theist, he is religious as well as good.**

This attempt to demonstrate a natural bond between morals and faith will be regarded by many as visionary and academic; some, however, think such a connection is manifest enough in the nature and history of man.   In certain quarters, no doubt, it is stoutly maintained that ethics and morality have really very little to do with religion, have originated apart from it, and can flourish without it. The separation can of course be effected in lecture-room or treatise, but scarcely in man as we have him, nor in practical life. History and research show clearly that a religious bent is one of the earliest and commonest features in the psychism of man: his ethics and moralities, such as they were at the first and have since become, such as they are today amongst savages, have always been greatly influenced by respect for the gods who for the time were ruling. In this way, morality, ethics, and religion have become inextricably interwoven; they have grown up together and the result of their mutual interaction has become ingrained by heredity and time; the mischief is done and a separation is no longer possible. Physically, socially, ethically, religiously, the 19th century man is the outcome of the ages; he is heir of all his ancestors, and can no more escape from the results of their early and confirmed instincts and practices than the modern Englishman can elude the landing

of Julius Cæsar, or the American the arrival
of the 'Mayflower.' In tracing down the
ethical and moral history of man, the most
salient factor met with is probably the
influence of great teachers. Plato, Socrates,
Confucius, Zoroaster, Gotama, Mohammed,
have moulded the ethics of large masses of
men ; but for Europe and America, Moses
and Christus far outweigh the rest put
together. Under any circumstances, the
historian of ethics and morals knows well
that the influence of theo-christianity is
incradicable. Gibbon, in his celebrated
15th chapter, disparages it, yet it is note-
worthy how frequently his great history is
occupied in recording the struggles and
successes of this very Faith. We believe
with most people that it has come to stay and
spread, but if it were extinguished tomorrow
it would leave its mark on the moral and
ethical evolution of man to the end of time.
Its impress would remain as distinct and
significant for the remote student of ethics, as
are the vermiform appendix of the intestine

and the disused muscles of the external ear for
the biologist of today, or the fossils of the rocks
for the geologist. Whatever be its short-
coming and blemish, few will deny that it
has sharpened the conscience of man, and
helped greatly to curb the vicious elements in
his nature. For western nations, it is at this
moment the most powerful moral antiseptic
which exists; its cleansing and purifying
action is beyond question. Moreover, if the
importance of religion in the making and
history of man be undeniable, equally so is
the part it plays in the making of his present-
day environment. It is useless to point to
the blameless life and high ethical standard
of individual men or small groups of men,
who, in casting aside all religious belief, have,
as they think, got entirely rid of its influence.
Such a situation is imaginary, is rendered
illusory by heredity and environment. These
estimable men remain, in spite of themselves,
under the momentum of good ancestry,
sometimes very good, and they breathe a
moral atmosphere to which religion is a large

contributor. How long would the momentum
last, if unrenewed; how long would the
atmosphere continue respirable, if religion
were totally eliminated? Fortunately, under
existing conditions the experiment cannot
be made. It was half-tried at the French
Revolution, and the result was not encouraging.
One minor sequence to any such venture may
perhaps be foreseen—however well a choice
few, with everything in their favour, might
conduct themselves, the masses of humanity,
with nothing better than a religionless
morality to guide and restrain them, would
soon learn to despise so feeble a mentor, and
would rise in lawless strength to take for
themselves whatever the classes refused to
give.

*   *   *   *   *

We must now leave the relations between
" Naturalism " and Supernaturalism to those
who are better able to deal with them. For
us, the two seem but different aspects of the
same truth ; obverse and reverse of a sterling,
though very human coinage. Supernaturalism

is not superstition. Religion will shake off
superstition—has, indeed, to a considerable
extent done so—even as astronomy has shed
astrology, and chemistry alchemy. But
neither religion nor naturalism can ever
dispense with super-nature. Possibly we are
as much mistaken as naturalist and supernaturalist at present consider each other to
be, but we plead, in the name of bewildered
onlookers, that cave as well as chancel should
have a hearing, and that mutual abuse should
cease. Meanwhile we gather up our scanty
but precious salvage, glad to find that even
so much can be rescued from the shipwreck
of former hopes and beliefs which the waves
and rocks of modern science and biblical
criticism have wrought. It is to secure this
remnant for ourselves, not to convince or
edify others, that these pages have been
written : we venture, however, to think they
voice the inarticulate broodings of many
who, like ourselves, have tried to eke out
an imperfect education with a smattering of
science. We can only hope that brighter

and better-furnished wits may be tempted to
take our data, or similar ones, and show they
can be made to yield a sounder position.   If
the stepping-stone we have attempted to lay
could once be rendered secure, it should not
be difficult for those who follow " Naturalism "
to pass on to the ground which Spencer offers
as the peaceful meeting-place of science and
religion.   In the last edition (1896) of his
" Principles   of   Sociology " (page 175),
Mr.   Spencer   concludes   his   chapter   on
" Religious Retrospect and Prospect " in the
following words :—

> "But one truth must grow ever
> clearer—the truth that there is an
> Inscrutable Existence everywhere
> manifested, to which he" (man of
> science) " can neither find nor conceive
> either beginning or end.   Amid
> the mysteries which become the
> more mysterious the more they are
> thought about, there will remain the
> one absolute certainty, that he is
> ever in presence of an Infinite and
> Eternal Energy, from which all things
> proceed."

This may be nothing more than a handful of that " metaphysical grass of transfigured Realism " with which Mr. Spencer has been said to " feed his lambs," but it may possibly appease certain wistful longings, which torment them, better than either the parched and garnered hay of science, or the tough roots of orthodox tradition. In suggesting that " Naturalism " and Supernaturalism, when rightly viewed, are complementary, and allies rather than foes, we are aware that our synthesis and apology will probably be rejected by both philosopher and theologian. To the last we may have to cry, with Goethe, for " more light "; but, for fellow-troglodytes and others, there is always hope from that Noumenal Light " which lighteth every man that cometh into the world." Whether the light come by way of an implanted religious instinct, or an evolved conscience, or through a special revelation, its source is the same.

Printed by TAYLOR & FRANCIS, Red Lion Court, Fleet Street, E.C.

www.ingramcontent.com/pod-product-compliance
Lightning Source LLC
Chambersburg PA
CBHW030842270326
41928CB00007B/1178